JEP
A BOEING COMPANY

GUIDED FLIGHT DISCOVERY
PRIVATE PILOT
MANEUVERS

Jeppesen
55 Inverness Drive East
Englewood, CO 80112-5498
Web site: www.jeppesen.com
Email: Captain@jeppesen.com
Copyright © Jeppesen
All Rights Reserved.
Published 1997-2007, 2011, 2012, 2013, 2014, 2018
Printed in the United States of America

Preface

The Guided Flight Discovery Pilot Training System emphasizes an application-oriented approach to pilot training. *Private Pilot Maneuvers* exemplifies this philosophy. When used in conjunction with the other components of the system, this manual provides an effective means to prepare for your flight training. The maneuvers are numbered for ease of reference and are grouped into categories based on similar operational characteristics. The categories are organized to present the maneuvers in the chronological order in which they are typically introduced. However, you can study and review the maneuvers in any order you desire. An effective strategy is to study the specific maneuvers assigned for the next flying lesson. Then, after practicing the maneuvers in flight, review the procedures to help you self-critique your performance.

Private Pilot Maneuvers is designed to lay flat for ease of study and instruction, whether you are on the ground or in flight. Each maneuver is presented using graphics, step-by-step procedure descriptions, and skill enhancement guidance. The photos and illustrations depict a variety of training airplanes and the terminology used in the procedure descriptions refers to some configuration/component differences, such as control stick vs. control wheel, fixed gear vs. retractable gear, and elevator vs. stabilator. However, the basic steps to perform the maneuver are the same regardless of the airplane you fly.

For each maneuver, the applicable excerpt from the FAA *Private Pilot — Airplane Airman Certification Standards (ACS)* is included. The skills element of each ACS maneuver task is explored in the step-by-step procedures and many of the knowledge and risk management elements are covered in the maneuver introductions, skill enhancement guidance, and in content following the step-by-step procedure. The FAA makes minor revisions to the ACS on a regular basis that you can access online.

 QR codes link you to animations in the Jeppesen Private Pilot online course. Just scan the code with your smart phone or tablet to view an overview of each maneuver. This overview is just a small sample of what the Private Pilot online course offers. To gain access to *all* of this course, including detailed step-by-step treatment of each maneuver plus in-flight video that shows what each maneuver looks like from the pilot's seat, scan the code on this page to go to JeppDirect where you can purchase the Jeppesen Private Pilot online course.

For more information about using this manual's learning tools, refer to the section, *How the Manual Works*, starting on page vi.

Table of Contents

TABLE OF CONTENTS ■ **Private Pilot Maneuvers**

How the Manual Works

Private Pilot Maneuvers uses innovative graphics and step-by-step procedure descriptions to help you visualize and understand each maneuver that you will perform in the airplane during training. For each maneuver, skill enhancement insets provide additional guidance, ACS insets provide FAA performance standards, and exercises let you test your comprehension. To get the most out of this material, review the following descriptions of the major design elements of this manual.

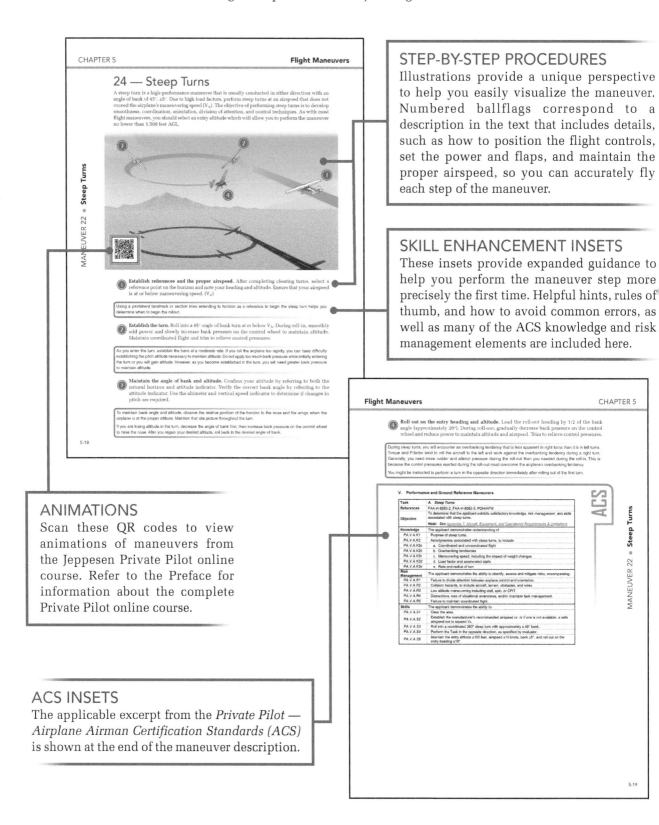

STEP-BY-STEP PROCEDURES

Illustrations provide a unique perspective to help you easily visualize the maneuver. Numbered ballflags correspond to a description in the text that includes details, such as how to position the flight controls, set the power and flaps, and maintain the proper airspeed, so you can accurately fly each step of the maneuver.

SKILL ENHANCEMENT INSETS

These insets provide expanded guidance to help you perform the maneuver step more precisely the first time. Helpful hints, rules of thumb, and how to avoid common errors, as well as many of the ACS knowledge and risk management elements are included here.

ANIMATIONS

Scan these QR codes to view animations of maneuvers from the Jeppesen Private Pilot online course. Refer to the Preface for information about the complete Private Pilot online course.

ACS INSETS

The applicable excerpt from the *Private Pilot — Airplane Airman Certification Standards (ACS)* is shown at the end of the maneuver description.

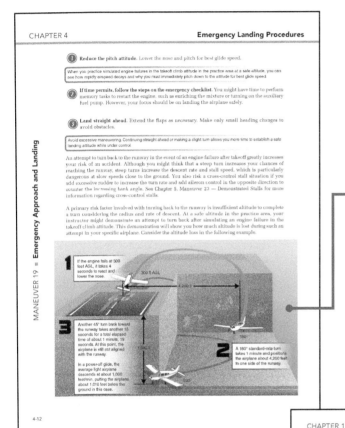

CHAPTER 4 — Emergency Landing Procedures

1 **Reduce the pitch attitude.** Lower the nose and pitch for best glide speed.

When you practice simulated engine failures in the takeoff climb attitude in the practice area at a safe altitude, you can see how rapidly airspeed decays and why you must immediately pitch down to the attitude for best glide speed.

2 **If time permits, follow the steps on the emergency checklist.** You might have time to perform memory tasks to restart the engine, such as enriching the mixture or turning on the auxiliary fuel pump. However, your focus should be on landing the airplane safely.

3 **Land straight ahead.** Extend the flaps as necessary. Make only small heading changes to avoid obstacles.

Avoid excessive maneuvering. Continuing straight ahead or making a slight turn allows you more time to establish a safe landing attitude while under control.

An attempt to turn back to the runway in the event of an engine failure after takeoff greatly increases your risk of an accident. Although you might think that a steep turn increases your chances of reaching the runway, steep turns increase the descent rate and stall speed, which is particularly dangerous at slow speeds close to the ground. You also risk a cross-control stall situation if you add excessive rudder to increase the turn rate and add aileron control in the opposite direction to counter the increasing bank angle. See Chapter 5, Maneuver 23 — Demonstrated Stalls for more information regarding cross-control stalls.

A primary risk factor involved with turning back to the runway is insufficient altitude to complete a turn considering the radius and rate of descent. At a safe altitude in the practice area, your instructor might demonstrate an attempt to turn back after simulating an engine failure in the takeoff climb attitude. This demonstration will show you how much altitude is lost during such an attempt in your specific airplane. Consider the altitude loss in the following example.

4-12

INNOVATIVE GRAPHICS

The illustrations and photos used throughout the manual are designed to enhance your learning experience and make difficult concepts easy to understand.

EXERCISES

Exercises follow each of the eight tabbed categories to help you evaluate your understanding of each maneuver presented. Answers are provided at the end of the manual.

CHAPTER 1 — Ground Operations

3 — TAXIING

The following questions pertain to a tricycle gear airplane.

1. True/False. Taxi speed is primarily controlled by using the brakes.

2. Does the effectiveness of the aileron, rudder, and elevator/stabilator controls increase or decrease as the airplane's speed decreases? _____

3. What action is helpful in reducing the radius of a turn while taxiing?

4. How would you position the flight controls for the surface wind conditions depicted in illustration A?

5. How would you position the flight controls for the surface wind conditions depicted in illustration B?

4 — BEFORE TAKEOFF CHECK

1. List at least two actions you should take when positioning the airplane to perform the before-takeoff check?

2. True/False. If the altimeter setting is not available during the before-takeoff check, you can adjust the altimeter to agree with field elevation.

3. Which is a step in the before takeoff check?
   A. Position the elevator trim to the full up position to reduce the back pressure necessary for takeoff.
   B. Turn on the fuel pump and set the mixture to RICH until a stable fuel flow is indicated on the fuel flow indicator (usually 3 to 5 seconds).
   C. Ensure the RPM drop with the magneto switch on the RIGHT and LEFT position does not exceed the maximum drop specified in the AFM/POH.

4. Name at least two engine/system indications that you must verify are in the green sector/arc.

5. Unless you are assigned a discrete transponder code, what code should you use for VFR flight?

1-28

CHAPTER 1

Ground Operations

Because ground operations vary from one airplane to another, the procedures in this section are intentionally general in nature. Therefore, you always must use an appropriate checklist that provides a logical step-by-step sequence for each task you will perform.

1 — Preflight Inspection

As a pilot, you are the final authority regarding the airworthiness and safe operation of your airplane. Your flight instructor will point out the various components to be inspected and explain how to determine the airplane's airworthiness. In addition, the airplane flight manual (AFM)/ pilot's operating handbook (POH) normally contains a checklist and other information regarding the preflight inspection. You must be able to identify, assess, and mitigate the risks associated with any discrepancy you find during the airplane inspection. You might need to enlist an aviation maintenance technician to answer questions or resolve problems that you find while inspecting the airplane.

The FAA expects all the equipment on the airplane to be operational before you fly—the condition under which the airplane was certified as airworthy. However, because some equipment is nonessential for safe operation of the airplane, the FAA has published procedures for flying with certain inoperative equipment. If a minimum equipment list (MEL) exists for your airplane, you must use it. The MEL takes into consideration the regulations and the specific requirements for your airplane and flight operation and indicates the equipment that is allowed to be inoperative for a particular flight. Because MELs are not common for light single-engine piston-powered airplanes, you will most likely use the procedure described in FAR 91.213. Refer to the Jeppesen *Private Pilot* textbook for more information regarding the procedures for flying with inoperative equipment.

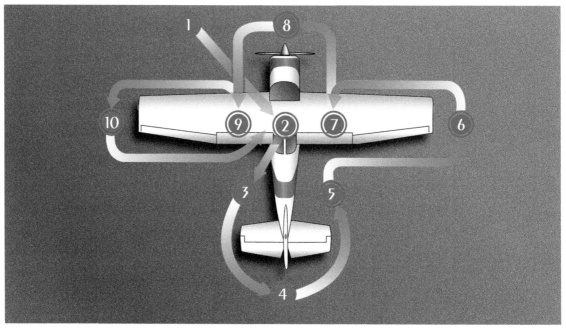

Prior to performing a visual inspection of the airplane, you should check the airplane logbooks and records to ensure that the appropriate airworthiness directives have been complied with, maintenance requirements have been met, and airplane inspections have been performed. Airworthiness directives (ADs) are issued to correct unsafe conditions in equipment that might exist or develop after the FAA issues an airworthiness certificate. ADs also prescribe the conditions under which the affected equipment may continue to be operated. Records of AD compliance and the airplane logbooks are not required to be on board the airplane.

① APPROACHING THE AIRPLANE

- Look for general discrepancies to the airplane components and structure such as misalignment of the landing gear, a low/flat tire, wrinkling/buckling of the skin, or damage to the wings, fuselage, and tail.

- Check for any staining, dripping, or puddles of fuel or oils.

- During the winter months, check for frost, snow, and ice on the airplane surfaces. Remove all of these contaminants.

IN CABIN

- Verify that all the required paperwork is on board the airplane. Use the acronym **ARROW** to help you remember the required documents.

    ○ **A**irworthiness certificate (FAR 91.203)

    ○ **R**egistration certificate (FAR 91.203)

    ○ **R**adio station class license (required by the Federal Communications Commission when transmitting to ground stations outside the United States)

    ○ **O**perating limitations, which may be in the form of an FAA-approved airplane flight manual and/or pilot's operating handbook (AFM/POH), placards, instrument markings, or any combination thereof. (FAR 91.9)

    ○ **W**eight and balance data, as well as an equipment list

- Ensure that the airplane has a compass deviation card (FAR 23.1547).
- Remove the control lock and check the controls for freedom of movement.
- Turn the master switch on.
- Verify the primary flight display (PFD) is on, if applicable.
- Verify the proper operation of fuel gauges and note the fuel quantity in each tank.
- Based on the airplane's checklist, confirm the function of specified electrical components, such as annunciators, the avionics fan, and flaps.
- Turn the master switch off.
- Inspect the instrument panel for any irregularities, such as cracked glass or any equipment that might have been removed for maintenance.
- Ensure the windscreen and windows are clean and in good condition.
- Before continuing to the exterior inspection, verify that the magneto switch, master switch, mixture control, and throttle are in the off position.

 FUSELAGE (LEFT SIDE)

- Moving toward the tail, visually inspect the left side of the fuselage for skin wrinkles or bubbles, dents, and loose rivets.

> External damage, such as wrinkled skin can indicate internal structural damage. Inspect around rivet heads for cracked paint or a black-oxide film that forms when a rivet works free in its hole.

- Check the lower surface of the fuselage for evidence of engine oil leakage, dents, and general condition.
- If a static port is located on the fuselage, check for obstructions.

> During cleaning or waxing of the airplane, the static port can become plugged. Ensure that the static source is open for proper operation of the airspeed indicator, altimeter, and vertical speed indicator.

- Ensure any antennas are attached securely and are in good condition.
- Verify the baggage door is closed and locked. Close the rear door, if applicable.

> Defer securing the baggage door if you must retrieve or store items, such as the tow bar, later in the preflight process. In addition, if the airplane has a rear door, you might still need to load passengers. Consider adding these tasks to the end of the preflight checklist as a reminder.

 EMPENNAGE

- Remove the external rudder lock (if installed).
- Inspect the tail surfaces for general condition, looking closely for skin wrinkles or bubbles, dents, and loose rivets.

MANEUVER 1 ■ **Preflight Inspection**

> Inspect the skin along spar lines and attachment points where load-related stresses are concentrated. Spar lines are lateral rivet lines that extend across the horizontal stabilizer, vertical stabilizer, and wings.

- Examine the rudder for damage, loose hinge bolts, and freedom of movement.
- Closely inspect the control cables and stops for damage.
- Visually inspect the flashing beacon (if applicable), tail light, and any antennas located on the vertical stabilizer.
- Examine the elevator/stabilator trim tab, checking for security and general condition.
- For tailwheel airplanes, check the steering arms, cables, and springs for wear. Additionally, inspect the tire for wear, cuts, abrasions, and proper inflation.
- Remove the tail tiedown chain or rope.

(5) FUSELAGE (RIGHT SIDE)

- Inspect the right side fuselage, as before, looking for skin wrinkles or bubbles, dents, and loose rivets.
- Check the rear window(s) for damage.

(6) RIGHT WING

- Thoroughly inspect the wing flap for general condition and the flap hinges for security.
- If the flap track is visible, check to ensure it is in good condition and does not show unusual wear.
- Inspect the aileron surfaces for dents and skin wrinkles and the hinges for security, damage, and freedom of movement.
- Check the aileron pushrod or cables for security, damage, and tension.
- Check the right wingtip for damage and secure attachment, and inspect the right navigation light.

> On metal airplanes, ensure that wingtips, fairings, and non-structural covers fabricated out of thin fiberglass or plastic are in good condition. Cracks radiating from screw holes or curved edges might be stop-drilled to prevent crack progression. Cracks that have continued beyond a stop-drilled location or any new cracks that have formed can lead to in-flight failure.

- Examine the leading edge of the wing for dents or other damage.

> Look for damage caused by rocks, ice, birds, and or hangar rash incidents on the leading edges of the wing, horizontal stabilizer, and vertical stabilizer. Also, ensure you know the proper condition of any aerodynamic devices, such as stall fences, slots, or vortex generators, or deicing equipment, such as weeping wings and boots.

- Inspect the upper surface of the wing for wrinkles or bubbles and dents, which can indicate internal structural damage.

> When inspecting composite airplanes, delamination of spar to skin or other structural problems can be identified by bubbles, fine hair-line cracks, or changes in sound when gently tapping on the structure with a fingertip.

- Remove the fuel cap and visually check the fuel quantity. In addition to ensuring that the fuel quantity is sufficient for the proposed flight, verify that the fuel level agrees with the fuel quantity gauge indication that you observed earlier.
- Before replacing the fuel cap, inspect the rubber gasket for cracks or deterioration.
- Inspect the fuel vent for obstructions. Depending on the airplane, the fuel vent is located in the filler cap or located on the underside of the wing as a tube or recessed area.

> Checking the fuel tank vent is an essential part of a preflight assessment. If outside air is unable to enter the tank as fuel is drawn into the engine, the eventual result is fuel starvation and engine failure.

- Use your fuel tester to take a fuel sample from the fuel tank drain(s) and check the color to verify that the fuel is the proper grade. If water or other contaminants are found in the sample, continue draining fuel until there is no evidence of contamination.

> Observe the fuel sample against a white background so you can easily see the color of the fuel. Water can form in the fuel tanks from condensation of moisture in the air, or it might be present in the fuel added to the tanks. Water is heavier than aviation fuel and will settle to the bottom of the fuel tester.

- Remove the wing tiedown rope or chain.

LANDING GEAR (RIGHT SIDE)

- Inspect the skin around the attachment points of the main landing gear for dents and wrinkles.
- Examine the tire for proper inflation and the condition of the tread. Look for abnormal wear patterns, sidewall cracks, and damage, such as cuts, bulges, imbedded foreign objects, and flat spots that expose visible cord.

> Plies of nylon cord are imbedded in the tire's rubber with each layer angled to assure strength and balance.

- Ensure the wheel hub is free from cracks, corrosion, and rust, that all fasteners are secure, and that the air valve stem is straight, capped, and in good condition.
- Check the wheel fairing (if installed) for cracks, dents, and security.
- Inspect the brake pads for wear and the hydraulic brake lines for security and leaks.
- If your airplane is equipped with oleo struts, ensure proper strut inflation.

NOSE

- Check the cowling for security—look for loose, worn, missing, or damaged fasteners, rivets, and latches.
- If able, inspect the engine components for loose wires and clamps, worn hoses, and oil or fuel leaks.

> Depending on the airplane, inspecting inside the cowling might be difficult without using a flashlight, even during day operations.

- Determine the oil quantity by removing and reading the dipstick. Add oil if the level is below the minimum recommended by the manufacturer. Then, replace the dipstick and tighten it securely.
- Drain the fuel strainer or gascolator on the underside of the airplane. Take a fuel sample and check for contamination.

> Any water or contaminants should accumulate in the fuel strainer or gascolator, which is often the lowest point in the fuel system.

- Inspect the propeller and spinner for security and check the propeller for nicks and cracks.

> Propeller nicks can cause excessive stress in the metal and should be repaired by an aviation maintenance technician prior to flight.

- If your airplane has a constant-speed propeller, check for oil leaks.

> You can detect oil leaks around the seals of constant-speed propellers by observing oil streaks on the back side of the propeller blades or oil spots on the cowling or windscreen.

MANEUVER 1 ■ **Preflight Inspection**

- Check the alternator/generator drive belts (if accessible) for proper tension and signs of wear.
- Verify that engine air inlets are unobstructed and that the air filter (if applicable) is free from substantial dirt, restrictions, or excessive wear.
- Ensure the exhaust pipe is secure and is in good condition.
- Examine the nosewheel tire for proper inflation, cuts, abrasions, and condition of the tread.
  - Check the wheel fairing (if installed) for cracks, dents, and security.
  - Carefully inspect the nosewheel strut for proper inflation, leaks, and security.
  - Inspect the steering linkages for security and the shimmy damper for leaks or damage.
  - Check the cowl flaps (if installed) for security.
- Check the exterior surface of the windshield for cleanliness and general condition.

> To clean the windshield, use a clean soft cloth and a cleaning compound specifically designed for airplane windshields. Do not use a dry rag because it can scratch the windshield surface.

- If a static port is located on the cowling, check for obstructions.

⑨ LANDING GEAR (LEFT SIDE)

- Examine the left main landing gear as you did the right main gear.

⑩ LEFT WING

- Inspect the left wing as you did the right wing.
- Examine the pitot tube for damage and check the opening for obstructions.

> A plugged pitot tube opening will cause the airspeed indicator to malfunction.

- If the static port is located on the pitot tube, ensure it is clean and free of obstructions.
- Test the stall warning system for proper function.

> Stall warning systems normally measure pressure distribution or angle of attack. Ensure you understand how the system in your airplane functions and how to check for proper operation.

II. Preflight Procedures

Task	A. Preflight Assessment
References	FAA-H-8083-2, FAA-H-8083-3, FAA-H-8083-23; POH/AFM; AC 00-6
Objective	To determine that the applicant exhibits satisfactory knowledge, risk management, and skills associated with preparing for safe flight.
Knowledge	The applicant demonstrates understanding of:
PA.II.A.K1	Pilot self-assessment.
PA.II.A.K2	Determining that the airplane to be used is appropriate and airworthy.
PA.II.A.K3	Airplane preflight inspection including:
PA.II.A.K3a	a. Which items must be inspected
PA.II.A.K3b	b. The reasons for checking each item
PA.II.A.K3c	c. How to detect possible defects
PA.II.A.K3d	d. The associated regulations
PA.II.A.K4	Environmental factors including weather, terrain, route selection, and obstructions.
Risk Management	The applicant demonstrates the ability to identify, assess and mitigate risks, encompassing:
PA.II.A.R1	Pilot.
PA.II.A.R2	Aircraft.
PA.II.A.R3	Environment (e.g., weather, airports, airspace, terrain, obstacles).
PA.II.A.R4	External pressures.
PA.II.A.R5	Aviation security concerns.
Skills	The applicant demonstrates the ability to:
PA.II.A.S1	Inspect the airplane with reference to an appropriate checklist.
PA.II.A.S2	Verify the airplane is in condition for safe flight and conforms to its type design.

MANEUVER 1 ■ **Preflight Inspection**

2 — Engine Starting

Although engine starting procedures can vary from one make and model of airplane to another, some safety precautions are common to most general aviation airplanes. You should avoid starting the engine with the tail of the airplane pointed toward people standing nearby, property on the ramp, open hangers, or other aircraft that could be damaged by the wind blast from the propeller. Inspect the ground under the propeller before you start the engine, especially if you are operating on an unimproved surface. Rocks, pebbles, or any other loose debris can be picked up by the propeller and cause damage to the blades or be hurled backward.

Engine staring procedures vary among airplanes so follow the appropriate checklist and expanded procedures in the AFM/POH. In cold weather—when air temperatures are below 20°F (-6°C)—the AFM/POH typically recommends using an external preheater and/or an external power source to start the engine.

STARTING A FUEL-INJECTED ENGINE

In a fuel-injected engine, the fuel is not vaporized until it is sprayed directly into the hot engine intakes. The general steps for a starting a fuel-injected engine in a typical training airplane are shown here.

① **Open the throttle.** Move the throttle forward approximately 1/8 to 1/2 inch depending on the checklist in the AFM/POH.

② **Ensure that the mixture is set to LEAN (IDLE CUTOFF).**

③ **Clear the area.** Verify that all people and equipment are a safe distance from the propeller. Open a window or the door, call out, "CLEAR," and listen for a response.

> Blowing debris can damage property or injure people so be aware of what is behind the airplane before starting the engine.

④ **Turn on the master switch.**

⑤ **Turn on the anti-collision lights.** Doing so provides a visual warning to people approaching the airplane that the engine is about to start.

⑥ **Prime the engine.** Turn on the fuel pump and set the mixture to RICH until a stable fuel flow is indicated on the fuel flow indicator (usually 3 to 5 seconds). Then set the mixture control to LEAN (IDLE CUTOFF) and turn the fuel pump off. If the engine is warm, the AFM/POH might direct you to omit priming.

> A strong fuel smell and difficultly starting the engine can occur if you have flooded the engine due to excessive priming. In this case, a typical starting procedure involves these actions: ensure the fuel pump is turned off, set the mixture to LEAN (IDLE CUTOFF), and open the throttle 1/2 to full before turning the ignition. When the engine starts, set the mixture to RICH and close the throttle promptly.

⑦ **Turn or press the ignition switch to engage the starter.** Advance the mixture control to RICH as the engine fires. To avoid damage to the starter, return the switch to the BOTH position as soon as the engine starts.

> The service life of an engine starter motor is drastically shortened from high heat through overuse so avoid continuous starter operation for periods longer than 30 seconds without a cool down period of at least 30 seconds to 1 minute. Some AFM/POHs specify times greater than these.

⑧ **Adjust the throttle to the recommended power setting.**

> In general, 1,000 RPM is recommended following engine start to allow oil pressure to rise and minimize undue engine wear due to insufficient lubrication at high RPM.

⑨ **Check the oil pressure.** If the oil pressure does not register in the normal range within 30 seconds in warm weather or within 60 seconds in cold weather, immediately shut down the engine to prevent possible damage.

MANEUVER 2 ■ Engine Starting

STARTING A CARBURETED ENGINE

The carburetor mixes the incoming air with fuel and delivers it to the combustion chamber. A float-type carburetor system is used on many light airplanes. To combat ice, engines with carburetors have a carburetor heat system designed to eliminate ice by routing air across a hot surface before it enters the carburetor. In addition, most gravity-feed, and some fuel-pump systems incorporate a manually operated pump called a primer. It is used to pump fuel directly into the intake system prior to engine start. The primer is useful in cold weather when fuel in the carburetor is difficult to vaporize. The general steps for a starting a carbureted engine in a typical training airplane are shown here.

MANEUVER 2 ■ **Engine Starting**

(1) **Prime the engine.** Use the engine primer to pump fuel into the intake system.

The number of primer strokes required depends on the length of time the engine has been shut down and the temperature of the outside air. In cold weather, a greater number of primer strokes might be necessary than when operating in warmer temperatures. Refer to your airplane's AFM/POH for the manufacturer's recommendation.

(2) **Set the carburetor heat control to COLD.**

(3) **Open the throttle.** Move the throttle forward approximately 1/8 to 1/2 inch depending on the checklist in the AFM/POH.

(4) **Set the mixture control to RICH.**

⑤ Clear the area. Ensure that all people and equipment are a safe distance from the propeller.

Blowing debris can damage property or injure people so be aware of what is behind the airplane before starting the engine.

⑥ Turn on the master switch.

⑦ Turn on the anti-collision lights. Doing so provides a visual warning to people approaching the airplane that the engine is about to start.

⑧ Turn or press the ignition switch to engage the starter. To avoid damage to the starter, return the switch to the BOTH position as soon as the engine starts.

The service life of an engine starter motor is drastically shortened from high heat through overuse so avoid continuous starter operation for periods longer than 30 seconds without a cool down period of at least 30 seconds to 1 minute. Some AFM/POHs specify times greater than these.

⑨ Adjust the throttle to the recommended power setting.

In general, 1,000 RPM is recommended following engine start to allow oil pressure to rise and minimize undue engine wear due to insufficient lubrication at high RPM.

⑩ Check the oil pressure. If the oil pressure does not register in the normal range within 30 seconds in warm weather or within 60 seconds in cold weather, immediately shut down the engine to prevent possible damage.

II. **Preflight Procedures**

Task	C. *Engine Starting*
References	FAA-H-8083-2, FAA-H-8083-3, FAA-H-8083-25; POH/AFM
Objective	To determine that the applicant exhibits satisfactory knowledge, risk management, and skills associated with recommended engine starting procedures.
Knowledge	The applicant demonstrates understanding of:
PA.II.C.K1	Starting under various conditions.
PA.II.C.K2	Starting the engine(s) by use of external power.
PA.II.C.K3	Engine limitations as they relate to starting.
Risk Management	The applicant demonstrates the ability to identify, assess and mitigate risks, encompassing:
PA.II.C.R1	Propeller safety.
Skills	The applicant demonstrates the ability to:
PA.II.C.S1	Position the airplane properly considering structures, other aircraft, wind, and the safety of nearby persons and property.
PA.II.C.S2	Complete the appropriate checklist.

MANEUVER 2 ■ **Engine Starting**

MANEUVER 3 ■ **Taxiing**

3 — Taxiing

To become proficient at taxiing, you must learn directional control techniques and how to use the power to control speed. Light training airplanes typically have either a steerable nosewheel linked to the rudder pedals or a castering nosewheel, and have disc brakes located on the main wheels. To stop or slow the airplane in a straight line, apply equal pressure on both the left and right brakes by pressing on the top of each rudder pedal. Apply differential braking to help steer the airplane while taxiing. Use the ailerons to counteract the effects of wind. Refer to the AFM/POH and the appropriate checklist for specific taxi procedures for your airplane.

In addition to controlling the airplane, you must maintain situational awareness while taxiing to prevent a runway incursion. A runway incursion is an occurrence at an airport involving an airplane, vehicle, person, or object on the ground that creates a collision hazard or results in the loss of proper separation with an aircraft taking off or landing. Prior to taxi, use an airport diagram to become familiar with the ramp and taxi environment, including runway incursion hot spots. Complete as many checklist items as possible before taxi or while holding short. At a towered airport, read back (in full) all clearances involving active runway crossing, hold short, or line up and wait instructions.

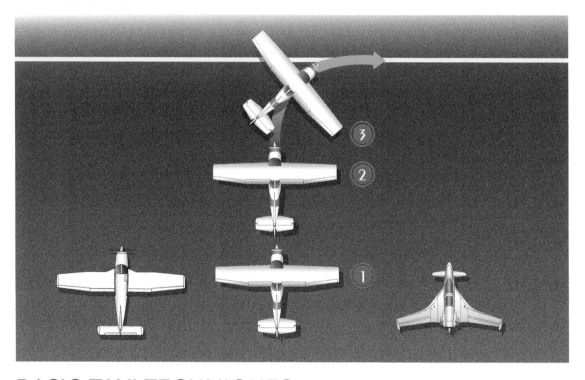

BASIC TAXI TECHNIQUES

 Clear the area around the airplane. Add power slowly until the airplane begins rolling and then reduce power. More power is required to start the airplane rolling than is required to keep it rolling.

A higher power setting is necessary to start and sustain an airplane in motion on a soft surface, such as grass, than on a hard surface.

 Test the brakes for proper operation. Readjust the power setting to obtain a normal taxi speed. Control taxi speed primarily by the throttle and secondarily by the brakes. Use the brakes only when a reduction of engine RPM is not sufficient to slow the airplane.

Continually riding the brakes to control speed while taxiing can cause excessive wear or overheating.

 Use the rudder pedals to steer. Press the right rudder pedal to turn the airplane to the right and the left rudder pedal to turn to the left. It is recommended that you taxi no faster than a brisk walk. In a confined area, taxi at a speed slow enough to enable you to stop by reducing the power or by shutting down the engine in the event of a brake failure.

Because the brakes can be controlled separately, applying the left or right brake in the direction of a turn can be helpful in reducing the turn radius.

Ensure you are familiar with airport markings, signs, and lights. If unsure of your position on the airport, stop and refer to an airport diagram or a moving map display. At a towered airport, you can request progressive taxi instructions.

TAXIING IN HEADWINDS

While taxiing in moderate or strong wind conditions, you must use special techniques to maintain airplane control. The aileron, rudder, and elevator/stabilator controls are relatively ineffective at slow speeds. However, as the speed of air over the control surfaces increases, control effectiveness also increases. The control surfaces respond the same, whether the airplane is taxiing at 5 knots with no wind or is stationary with a 5-knot headwind. However, if you taxi the airplane at 15 knots into a 15-knot wind, the control surfaces have a 30-knot airflow over them and respond to that airflow velocity.

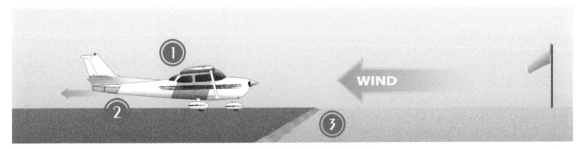

WIND

 Position the ailerons. Hold the control wheel to maintain the ailerons in a neutral or level position.

When taxiing directly into a headwind the airplane has little or no tendency to tip because the wind flows over and under both wings equally.

 Position the elevator/stabilator. Apply neutral or slightly forward pressure on the control wheel to maintain the elevator/stabilator in a neutral or slightly down position and exert normal pressure on the nose gear.

Holding too much forward pressure on the control wheel while taxiing into a strong headwind forces the tail up and the nose down. This increases the load placed on the nose gear, compresses the nose strut, and puts the propeller closer to the ground. Although normally this forward pressure does not create a hazard, on rough or uneven terrain the likelihood of a propeller strike increases.

 Taxi over rough ground. Hold the control wheel aft to raise the elevator/stabilator. This procedure forces the tail down and increases propeller clearance.

If the elevator/stabilator is incorrectly positioned downward, the wind can raise the tail causing the airplane to have a tendency to tip or nose over.

MANEUVER 3 ■ **Taxiing**

QUARTERING HEADWINDS

In a strong quartering headwind, the wind has a tendency to get under the upwind wing and tip the airplane toward the downwind side. If you do not properly position the ailerons, the upwind wing can be lifted, which can cause directional control problems or even overturn the airplane. In addition, wind striking the rudder can cause the airplane to turn into the wind. Improper elevator/stabilator position can reduce nosewheel friction and increase this weathervaning tendency.

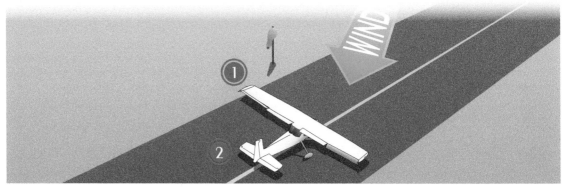

① **Position the ailerons.** Fully turn the control wheel in the direction of the wind placing the upwind aileron in the up position. Fully deflect the ailerons due to reduced control effectiveness at slow taxi speeds.

② **Position the elevator/stabilator.** Hold the control wheel to maintain the elevator/stabilator in a neutral or level position. A neutral elevator position helps maintain sufficient nosewheel friction and enables positive directional control.

TAXIING IN TAILWINDS

The effectiveness of the control surfaces also is influenced by tailwinds. For example, if you taxi the airplane at 5 knots with a tailwind of 5 knots, the taxi speed and the wind speed are canceled, and the control surfaces respond as though no wind exists. If you slow the airplane, the control surfaces respond as though there were an increasing tailwind component. When you stop the airplane completely, the control surfaces are subjected to the direct effects of a 5-knot tailwind.

① **Position the ailerons.** Hold the control wheel to maintain the ailerons in a neutral or level position.

② **Position the elevator/stabilator.** Hold the control wheel full forward to maintain the elevator/stabilator in a full down position. This control position causes the wind to strike the upper surface of the elevator/stabilator and to exert a downward force on the tail.

In a strong tailwind you might need to reduce the throttle to idle to control your taxi speed. Taxiing in a tailwind usually requires less engine power because the wind has a tendency to push the airplane, increasing taxi speed.

MANEUVER 3 ■ Taxiing

QUARTERING TAILWINDS

A quartering tailwind is the most critical wind condition for taxiing a tricycle gear, high-wing airplane. Because quartering tailwinds have a tendency to flow beneath the elevator/stabilator and lift the tail, the airplane can tip over on the nosewheel and one main wheel.

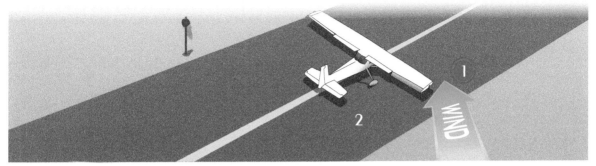

① Position the ailerons. Fully turn the control wheel in the direction away from the wind. In a right quartering tailwind, turn the control wheel fully to the left, or left aileron up. Reverse the position of the aileron control when taxiing with a left quartering tailwind.

② Position the elevator/stabilator. Hold the control wheel fully forward to maintain the elevator/stabilator in a down position to counteract the airplane's tipping tendency.

Be particularly cautious when you are slowing down and beginning a turn in a quartering tailwind. The increasing tailwind component, combined with the normal tendency of the airplane to tip during the turn, makes the airplane especially vulnerable to being overturned. Slow taxi speeds and slow turns minimize this danger.

MANEUVER 3 ▪ **Taxiing**

ACS

II. Preflight Procedures

Task	D. Taxiing (ASEL, AMEL)
References	FAA-H-8083-2, FAA-H-8083-3, FAA-H-8083-25; POH/AFM; AC 91-73; Chart Supplements; AIM
Objective	To determine that the applicant exhibits satisfactory knowledge, risk management, and skills associated with safe taxi operations, including runway incursion avoidance.
Knowledge	The applicant demonstrates understanding of:
PA.II.D.K1	Current airport aeronautical references and information resources including Chart Supplements, airport diagram, and appropriate references.
PA.II.D.K2	Taxi instructions/clearances.
PA.II.D.K3	Airport markings, signs, and lights.
PA.II.D.K4	Visual indicators for wind.
PA.II.D.K5	Aircraft lighting.
PA.II.D.K6	Procedures for:
PA.II.D.K6a	a. Appropriate flight deck activities prior to taxi, including route planning and identifying the location of Hot Spots
PA.II.D.K6b	b. Radio communications at towered and nontowered airports
PA.II.D.K6c	c. Entering or crossing runways
PA.II.D.K6d	d. Night taxi operations
PA.II.D.K6e	e. Low visibility taxi operations
Risk Management	The applicant demonstrates the ability to identify, assess and mitigate risks, encompassing:
PA.II.D.R1	Inappropriate activities and distractions.
PA.II.D.R2	Confirmation or expectation bias as related to taxi instructions.
PA.II.D.R3	A taxi route or departure runway change.
Skills	The applicant demonstrates the ability to:
PA.II.D.S1	Receive and correctly read back clearances/instructions, if applicable.
PA.II.D.S2	Use an airport diagram or taxi chart during taxi, if published, and maintain situational awareness.
PA.II.D.S3	Position the flight controls for the existing wind conditions.
PA.II.D.S4	Complete the appropriate checklist.
PA.II.D.S5	Perform a brake check immediately after the airplane begins moving.
PA.II.D.S6	Maintain positive control of the airplane during ground operations by controlling direction and speed without excessive use of brakes
PA.II.D.S7	Comply with airport/taxiway markings, signals, and ATC clearances and instructions.
PA.II.D.S8	Position the airplane properly relative to hold lines.

4 — Before Takeoff Check

The before takeoff check is an integral part of every flight. Use the Before-Takeoff checklist in the AFM/POH to ensure that you check each item in the proper sequence and do not omit any items. After taxiing to the runup area, position the airplane so the propeller blast is not directed toward other aircraft, buildings, or vehicles. If possible, point the nose of the airplane into the wind to improve engine cooling. To prevent damage to the propeller and other parts of the airplane, avoid engine runups on loose gravel or sand. Divide your attention between your flight deck duties and outside the airplane. The before takeoff check can include, but is not limited to the following items.

1. **Set the parking brake.**

2. **Verify that the cabin doors are securely closed and locked/latched.**

Ensure that passengers who are sitting by doors know how to verify that the door is closed and locked/latched.

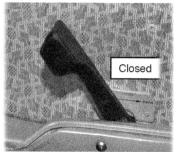

3. **Check the flight controls.** Move the controls to verify freedom of movement, full travel, and correct control surface deflection.

Check the flight controls throughout their entire operating range, including full aileron, elevator, and rudder deflection in all directions.

4. **Check and set the flight instruments.** Ensure instruments show the proper indications and that digital instruments (if applicable) do not display any red Xs.

> If the altimeter does not indicate the field elevation within 75 feet after you set the current altimeter setting, consider postponing the flight and alerting an aviation maintenance technician to the discrepancy.
>
> A quick taxi and run-up might not allow enough time for analog gyroscopic instruments to reach an acceptable RPM to indicate properly.

Verify the airspeed indicator reads zero.

The attitude indicator should be erect with the miniature airplane aligned with the horizon.

Set the altimeter to the current altimeter setting or to the correct field elevation.

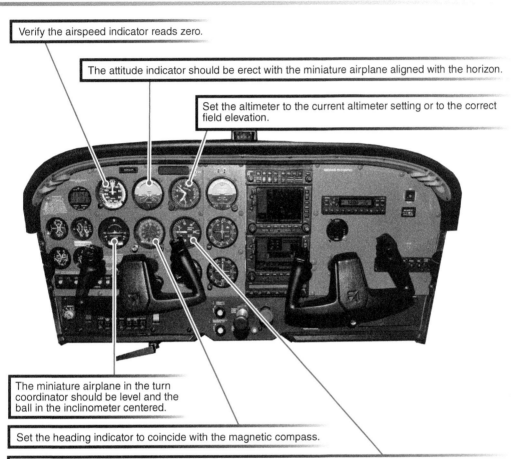

The miniature airplane in the turn coordinator should be level and the ball in the inclinometer centered.

Set the heading indicator to coincide with the magnetic compass.

Verify that the vertical speed indicator (VSI) reads zero. If the VSI does not read zero, you can use the value shown as the zero indication.

5. **Position the fuel selector valve.** Select the fullest tank or the BOTH position, as recommended by the AFM/POH.

6. **Set the mixture control.** Typically, airplane checklists indicate setting the mixture to RICH. However, at high altitude airports, you normally lean the mixture for smooth engine operation. Refer to the AFM/POH for the appropriate procedures.

7. **Set the trim.** Position the elevator trim and rudder trim (if installed) to the TAKEOFF position.

8. **Perform the runup.** Hold the brakes and add power to the RPM setting recommended by the manufacturer.

> If the airplane is equipped with a constant-speed propeller, cycle the propeller to verify proper operation. Typically, you reduce the RPM until a drop of 250 to 500 RPM is reached and then return to high RPM at least 3 times.

In a carburetor-equipped airplane, you position the carburetor heat control to ON and check for a corresponding drop in RPM and then return it to the COLD position. In some atmospheric conditions, carburetor ice can form while taxiing. If carburetor ice has formed, you might notice a larger initial drop in RPM followed by a slight increase in RPM. The initial drop might be accompanied by engine roughness that subsides with the RPM increase.

- **Check each magneto for proper operation.** Note the RPM with the magneto switch in the BOTH position, then move the magneto switch to the RIGHT position and note the RPM drop. Next, return the magneto switch to BOTH, then switch to the LEFT position and again note the RPM drop. Finally, return the magneto switch to the BOTH position for takeoff. The AFM/POH specifies the maximum permissible RPM drop for each magneto, as well as the maximum differential.

- **Check the engine and system indications.** Verify that the indications for items, such as oil temperature, oil pressure, fuel flow, vacuum pressure, and electrical charge, register in the green arc/sector.

In cold weather, oil temperature might not indicate in the normal range until after takeoff. Check the AFM/POH for acceptable indications prior to takeoff.

An electrical system discharge can indicate a faulty alternator, broken alternator belt, or excessive electrical load.

If the vacuum system is not functioning properly, the attitude indicator and heading indicator can display unreliable information.

- **Ensure no annunciators are illuminated.** Typical annunciations alert you to system conditions such as low oil pressure, low fuel quantity, and electrical system malfunctions.

9. **Reduce power.** Typically, the AFM/POH indicates a power setting at 1,000 RPM or below. Many checklists include verifying smooth engine operation with an idle power setting.

10. **Configure the avionics.** Based on the airplane's equipment and the flight requirements, set the communication frequencies, initial navigation sources and courses, autopilot preselects, heading and altitude bugs, and the transponder code.

Although you typically use the code 1200 for VFR flight, ATC might assign you a discrete code at certain airports, such as those in Class B and Class C airspace.

11. **Turn on the airplane lights.** Ensure your landing light, navigation lights, flashing beacon and/or strobe lights are on as required.

12. **Perform the takeoff briefing.** Include:

- Wind direction and velocity.
- Runway length.
- Takeoff distance.
- Initial heading.
- Initial altitude.
- Takeoff and climb speeds.
- Departure procedures.
- Emergency plan in case of an engine failure after takeoff.

II. Preflight Procedures

Task	F. Before Takeoff Check
References	FAA-H-8083-2, FAA-H-8083-3, FAA-H-8083-23; POH/AFM
Objective	To determine that the applicant exhibits satisfactory knowledge, risk management, and skills associated with the before takeoff check.
Knowledge	The applicant demonstrates understanding of:
PA.II.F.K1	Purpose of pre-takeoff checklist items including:
PA.II.F.K1a	a. Reasons for checking each item
PA.II.F.K1b	b. Detecting malfunctions
PA.II.F.K1c	c. Ensuring the airplane is in safe operating condition as recommended by the manufacturer
Risk Management	The applicant demonstrates the ability to identify, assess and mitigate risks, encompassing:
PA.II.F.R1	Division of attention while conducting pre-flight checks.
PA.II.F.R2	Unexpected runway changes by ATC.
PA.II.F.R3	Wake turbulence.
Skills	The applicant demonstrates the ability to:
PA.II.F.S1	Review takeoff performance.
PA.II.F.S2	Complete the appropriate checklist.
PA.II.F.S3	Properly position the airplane considering other aircraft, vessels, and wind.
PA.II.F.S4	Divide attention inside and outside the flight deck.
PA.II.F.S5	Verify that engine parameters and airplane configuration are suitable.

MANEUVER 4 ■ **Before Takeoff Check**

MANEUVER 4 ■ **Before Takeoff Check**

5 — Postflight Procedures

You maintain a high level of vigilance throughout a flight but remember, the flight is not over after you land—you still have several important tasks to perform as part of your postflight procedures. These tasks include completing the after landing and engine shutdown checklists, as well as parking and securing the airplane.

AFTER LANDING

After landing, gradually slow the airplane to normal taxi speed before turning off the runway. Use the checklist in the AFM/POH to perform the after landing check after you stop the airplane clear of the active runway. Some of the items can include:

- Set the power. Depending on the airplane, the after landing checklist might specify a power setting, such as 1,000 RPM. In addition, you might need to set the carburetor heat to COLD, move the propeller to full forward, or lean the mixture.

> In an airplane with a carburetor, moving the carburetor heat control to the COLD position prevents unfiltered air from being drawn into the carburetor, which can cause damage to the internal components of the engine.

- Turn off the fuel pump. The checklist for your airplane might have required you to turn on the auxiliary fuel pump prior to landing.
- Retract the flaps.
- Set the trim to the neutral or TAKEOFF position.
- Turn off any lights that are not required.
- Contact ground control or self-announce your intentions. At controlled (towered) airports, contact ground control for taxi clearance. At uncontrolled (nontowered) airports, transmit your position and intentions on the UNICOM or MULTICOM frequency.

> Ensure you follow proper taxi procedures after completing the after landing checklist. Read back the ATC taxi clearance, use an airport diagram or moving map display, and position the controls to compensate for wind.

PARKING AND SECURING

When taxiing into the parking area, use a safe taxi speed and follow any hand signals you receive from ramp personnel. In general, there are two ways to park an airplane. One way is to taxi the airplane into its designated parking spot, shut down and secure the engine, and then safely deplane any passengers. However, because of the proximity of other aircraft, this procedure might not be possible. In this situation, you should taxi the airplane near your intended parking spot and position the airplane so that the prop wash does not endanger people or property on the ramp. Then, shut down and secure the engine, safely deplane any passengers, and use a towbar to maneuver the airplane into parking. After you have positioned the airplane in its parking spot, you should tie down the airplane and perform a postflight inspection.

ENGINE SHUTDOWN

Most airplanes have specific procedures for engine shutdown. You should always follow the recommendations contained in the AFM/POH.

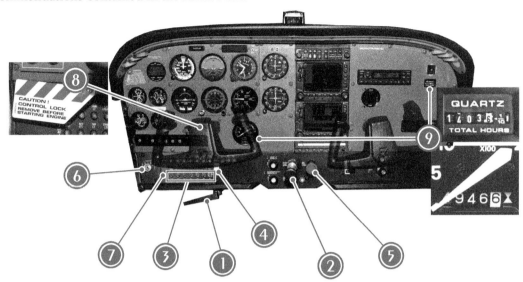

(1) Set the parking brake.

(2) Set the power to idle, or as recommended by the manufacturer.

(3) Turn off all electrical equipment.

(4) Turn off the avionics power switch.

(5) Set the mixture control to LEAN (IDLE CUTOFF)

(6) **Turn the ignition switch off when the engine stops.** As an added precaution, remove the key from the ignition.

(7) Turn the master switch off.

> In airplanes with integrated flight displays, you might need to note the tachometer time prior to turning off the master switch, and consequently, the digital engine instruments.

(8) Install the control lock.

(9) **Record the flight time.** Read the total engine time on the tachometer and the time from engine start to shutdown on the Hobbs meter.

> If you are renting an airplane, you are typically charged by the time on the Hobbs meter, which is also the flight time you log. The tach time is used to determine engine service time for maintenance and inspections, such as the 100-hour inspection.

MANEUVER 5 ▪ **Postflight Procedures**

SECURING

To secure the airplane, you must ensure the airplane is protected from damage due to high winds or gusty conditions, complete a postflight inspection so you can address any discrepancies for future flights, and lock the airplane to prevent unauthorized access.

1. **Park the airplane.** Release the parking brake, deplane any passengers, and position the airplane in the parking spot or hangar using a towbar, if necessary.

> If a towbar is not available, you can move the airplane by pushing on various components. For example, you can push on the leading edge of the horizontal and vertical stabilizers as long as you only apply pressure to the leading edge near the fuselage. The leading edge of the wing also is a good push point on low-wing airplanes if you are careful to only apply pressure at rib locations. On most high-wing airplanes, you can move the airplane by pushing on the wing struts.

> If hangaring the airplane, ensure that enough space is available so the airplane does not run into the hangar, another aircraft, equipment, or a vehicle.

2. **Place chocks in front of and behind the main wheels.**

3. **Secure the airplane with tiedown chains or ropes.** This step does not apply if the airplane is hangared.

> Tiedowns vary significantly from chains to well-worn ropes. Because chains are not flexible, avoid making them too taught. Allow the airplane some movement to prevent airframe structural damage.

4. **Install airplane protection equipment.** Place the pitot tube cover, cowling inlet covers, rudder gust locks, window sunscreens, and propeller security locks, as applicable.

> While performing parking and securing activities, ensure you are also monitoring any passengers that are waiting on the ramp.

5. **Complete a postflight inspection.** Check for oil and fuel streaks on the cowling, fuel stains under the wings, damage to the landing gear and tires, such as flat spots, and leaking hydraulic fluid near the brakes.

6. **Lock the airplane.** Remove all personal items and then close and lock all windows and doors, including the baggage door. Do not leave the keys in the airplane.

7. **Document any discrepancies.** Follow the appropriate procedure to record (squawk) any discrepancies that you discovered in flight or during the postflight inspection and ground the airplane, if necessary.

8. **Service the airplane.** If renting the airplane, follow the operator procedures for fueling the airplane.

> Filling the fuel tanks to prevent water condensation from forming inside the tank is typically a good practice. However, this practice might be discouraged by a rental operator in order to accommodate the next pilot who might desire a reduced fuel load.

XII. Postflight Procedures

Task	A. After Landing, Parking and Securing (ASEL, AMEL)
References	FAA-H-8083-2, FAA-H-8083-3; POH/AFM
Objective	To determine that the applicant exhibits satisfactory knowledge, risk management, and skills associated with after landing, parking, and securing procedures.
Knowledge	The applicant demonstrates understanding of:
PA.XII.A.K1	Airplane shutdown, securing, and postflight inspection.
PA.XII.A.K2	Documenting in-flight/postflight discrepancies.
Risk Management	The applicant demonstrates the ability to identify, assess and mitigate risks, encompassing:
PA.XII.A.R1	Inappropriate activities and distractions.
PA.XII.A.R2	Confirmation or expectation bias as related to taxi instructions.
PA.XII.A.R3	Airport specific security procedures.
PA.XII.A.R4	Disembarking passengers.
Skills	The applicant demonstrates the ability to:
PA.XII.A.S1	Demonstrate runway incursion avoidance procedures.
PA.XII.A.S2	Park in an appropriate area, considering the safety of nearby persons and property.
PA.XII.A.S3	Complete the appropriate checklist.
PA.XII.A.S4	Conduct a postflight inspection and document discrepancies and servicing requirements, if any.
PA.XII.A.S5	Secure the airplane.

MANEUVER 5 ▪ **Postflight Procedures**

MANEUVER 5 ■ **Postflight Procedures**

EXERCISES — GROUND OPERATIONS

1 — PREFLIGHT INSPECTION

1. Prior to performing a visual inspection of the airplane, you should check the airplane logbooks and records for what information?

2. What documents are required on board the airplane?

3. How can you tell when water is present in a fuel sample?

4. True/False. Nicks on the propeller can cause excessive stress and should be checked by a certificated mechanic.

5. Which are items to check on the wing during the preflight inspection?
   A. A fuel sample from the fuel tank drain and the fuel vents and pitot tube for blockage
   B. The fuel quantity and the elevator/stabilator for security, damage, and freedom of movement
   C. A fuel sample from the fuel strainer or gascolator and the aileron for security, damage and freedom of movement

2 — ENGINE STARTING

1. True/False. Before you start the engine, a thorough look around the propeller eliminates the need for opening a window or door and shouting "CLEAR!"

2. Which is a step in the starting procedure for a fuel-injected engine?
   A. Set the mixture to RICH prior to engaging the starter.
   B. Open the throttle to approximately 1/8 to 1/2 inch after the engine starts.
   C. Turn the ignition switch and then advance the mixture control to RICH as the engine fires.

3. What are two actions that you can take to help make it easier to start an engine in very cold weather?

4. After you start the engine in cold weather, the oil pressure should register properly within how many seconds? _____

5. After starting the engine, what action should you take in the event the oil pressure does not register within the green arc in the recommended time?

3 — TAXIING

The following questions pertain to a tricycle gear airplane.

1. True/False. Taxi speed is primarily controlled by using the brakes.

2. Does the effectiveness of the aileron, rudder, and elevator/stabilator controls increase or decrease as the airplane's speed decreases? _____

3. What action is helpful in reducing the radius of a turn while taxiing?

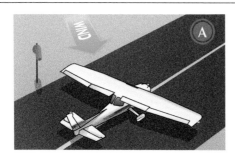 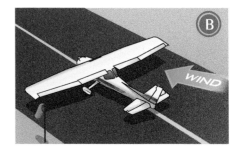

4. How would you position the flight controls for the surface wind conditions depicted in illustration A?

5. How would you position the flight controls for the surface wind conditions depicted in illustration B?

4 — BEFORE TAKEOFF CHECK

1. List at least two actions you should take when positioning the airplane to perform the before takeoff check?

2. True/False. If the altimeter setting is not available during the before takeoff check, you can adjust the altimeter to agree with field elevation.

3. Which is a step in the before takeoff check?
   A. Position the elevator trim to the full up position to reduce the back pressure necessary for takeoff.
   B. Turn on the fuel pump and set the mixture to RICH until a stable fuel flow is indicated on the fuel flow indicator (usually 3 to 5 seconds).
   C. Ensure the RPM drop with the magneto switch on the RIGHT and LEFT position does not exceed the maximum drop specified in the AFM/POH.

4. Name at least two engine/system indications that you must verify are in the green sector/arc.

5. Unless you are assigned a discrete transponder code, what code should you use for VFR flight?

5 — POSTFLIGHT PROCEDURES

1. Which is an action that might be included in an after landing checklist?
   A. Turn off the fuel pump; install the control lock.
   B. Retract the flaps; turn off all electrical equipment.
   C. Retract the flaps; contact ground control for a taxi clearance.

2. Name at least three actions that are included in the engine shutdown procedure.

   _____

   _____

3. True/False. You should install the control lock before engine shutdown.

4. If you move an airplane by pushing on the leading edge of a wing, where should you apply pressure?

   _____

5. Name at least two discrepancies that you should look for during a postflight inspection.

   _____

EXERCISES ■ **Ground Operations**

CHAPTER 2

Basic Maneuvers

6 — Straight-and-Level Flight

During straight-and-level flight you can maintain a constant heading and altitude by controlling the nose and wing positions with reference to the natural horizon. Although you can use the flight instruments as a cross-check to confirm that you are maintaining straight-and-level flight, your primary reference should be the horizon to the front and side of the airplane. Keeping your eyes primarily focused outside the flight deck also helps you see and avoid other aircraft.

Trimming eliminates the need for continuous forward or backward pressure on the control wheel to maintain attitude. If the airplane feels nose-heavy, you are holding back pressure to maintain a given attitude. Likewise, if forward pressure is required, the airplane feels tail-heavy. When the airplane is properly trimmed, you do not have to apply either forward or back pressure to maintain a constant pitch attitude. Use the trim tab only to remove pressure; do not use it to fly the airplane. The proper procedure is to set the airplane in the desired pitch attitude and at the selected airspeed, then trim away any control pressure necessary to hold that attitude. With a few exceptions, adjust the trim whenever you must apply a continuous forward or rearward force to the control wheel. The same principles apply if you have rudder trim in your airplane. However, you should also refer to the turn coordinator while trimming the rudder to help you maintain coordinated flight.

When you are introduced to straight-and-level flight (or any other maneuver), your instructor normally demonstrates the maneuver first, then passes the controls to you. To ensure that it is clear as to who has control of the airplane, the FAA strongly recommends that you use of a three-step process when exchanging the flight controls. During the preflight briefing, you should review with your instructor the following procedures for passing control of the airplane.

PILOT PASSING CONTROL: *"You have the flight controls."*

PILOT TAKING CONTROL: *"I have the flight controls."*

PILOT PASSING CONTROL: *"You have the flight controls."*

The pilot passing the controls should continue to fly until the pilot taking the controls acknowledges the exchange by saying, *"I have the flight controls."* Perform a visual check to ensure that the other pilot actually has the controls. At times, your instructor might need to assume control of the

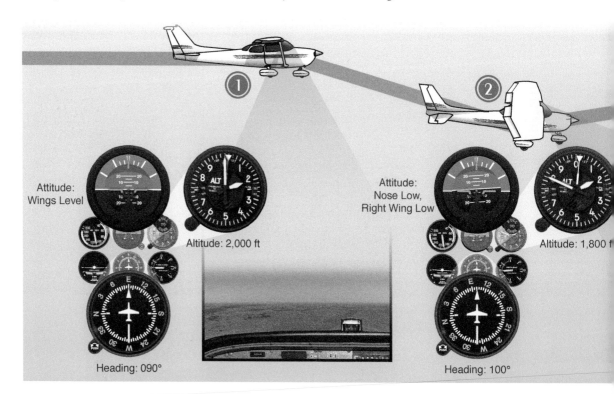

Attitude:
Wings Level

Altitude: 2,000 ft

Heading: 090°

Attitude:
Nose Low,
Right Wing Low

Altitude: 1,800 ft

Heading: 100°

airplane from you. In this case, your instructor should take the controls while informing you, *"I have the flight controls."*

 Establish the airplane on a specific heading and altitude. Adjust the rudder to maintain coordinated flight and trim to relieve control pressures.

- Maintain a wings-level position by keeping the wingtips a given distance above (high-wing airplane) or below (low-wing airplane) the horizon.
- By keeping a point on the airplane's nose or spot on the windshield in a fixed position in relation to a point on the horizon, you can maintain your desired altitude.

 Reestablish the airplane on the desired path after a deviation. Brief periods of inattention, power changes, turbulence, or wind gusts can cause the airplane to drift away from a desired course and altitude. After you detect a change in the position of your airplane's reference points in relation to the horizon, take these actions:

- Determine the magnitude of the deviation from the desired heading and altitude by cross-checking the flight instruments.
- Adjust the elevator/stabilator and ailerons to return to the original heading and altitude. Simultaneously adjust power to maintain the desired airspeed and trim to relieve control pressures.

 Maintain the heading and altitude. After you have returned to the desired heading and altitude, adjust the flight controls to maintain the proper wing and nose positions in relation to the horizon. Adjust power to maintain airspeed and trim to relieve control pressures.

Straight-and-Level Flight

The *Private Pilot Airman Certification Standards (ACS)* do not include specific criteria for straight-and-level flight using outside references. However, you can refer to the performance standards for straight-and-level flight solely by reference to instruments. See Maneuver 30 — Attitude Instrument Flying.

ACS

MANEUVER 6 ■ **Straight-and-Level Flight**

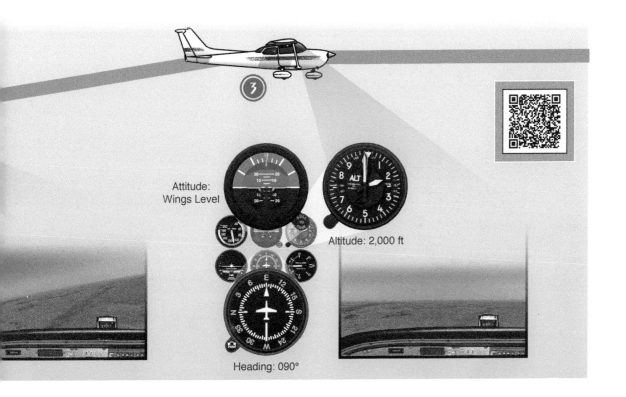

Attitude: Wings Level

Altitude: 2,000 ft

Heading: 090°

7 — Climbs

A climb is a basic maneuver designed to produce a gain in altitude. You must apply the appropriate control pressure to establish the proper climb attitude and learn how to use the trim to maintain the climb attitude. During training you practice a variety of climbs; some are constant-rate climbs and others are constant-airspeed climbs. You should know the engine power settings, natural horizon pitch attitudes, and flight instrument indications that produce climbs at these speeds:

- **Best angle-of-climb speed (V_X)**—the greatest altitude gain in the shortest distance.
- **Best rate-of-climb speed (V_Y)**—the most gain in altitude in the least amount of time.
- **Cruise climb speed**—used during cross-country flight while climbing to cruising altitude to provide a relatively higher groundspeed, better engine cooling, greater control authority, and increased visibility over the nose of the airplane.

(1) Establish the climb attitude. After clearing the airspace around the airplane, simultaneously add power and apply back pressure on the control stick. Add right rudder to compensate for the left-turning tendencies that result from the increase in pitch attitude and decrease in airspeed. Trim up elevator/stabilator and right rudder (if available).

(2) Maintain the climb attitude. Maintain airspeed and heading using outside references and instrument cross-checks. Adjust the pitch attitude to maintain airspeed and adjust bank angle to correct for heading deviations. If changes are necessary, make small adjustments, allow the airplane to stabilize, and then trim to relieve the control pressures.

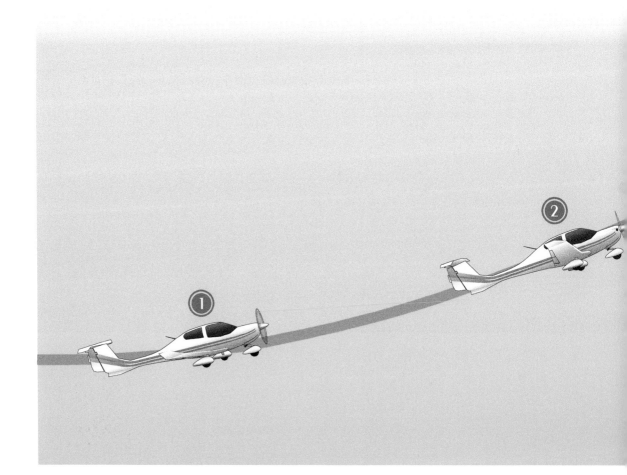

MANEUVER 7 ■ **Climbs**

Begin leveling off at the appropriate point. If you are climbing at 500 ft/min, return to straight-and-level flight by gradually lowering the nose approximately 50 feet prior to the desired leveloff altitude. Maintain climb power to accelerate to cruise speed.

> Generally, a 10% lead is sufficient for leveloff. For example, 10% of a 500 ft/min climb yields a 50-foot lead for leveloff.
>
> As the airplane accelerates, you need less right rudder pressure (or increasing left rudder pressure against the right rudder trim) as the left-turning tendencies diminish.

 Return to cruise flight. Reduce power to the cruise setting when the desired cruise speed is reached. Trim to relieve the control pressures and, if necessary, lean the mixture.

Climbs

The *Private Pilot Airman Certification Standards (ACS)* do not include specific criteria for climbs using outside references. However, you can refer to the performance standards for constant-airspeed climbs solely by reference to instruments. See Maneuver 30 — Attitude Instrument Flying.

MANEUVER 7 ■ **Climbs**

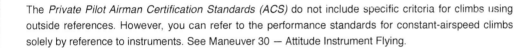

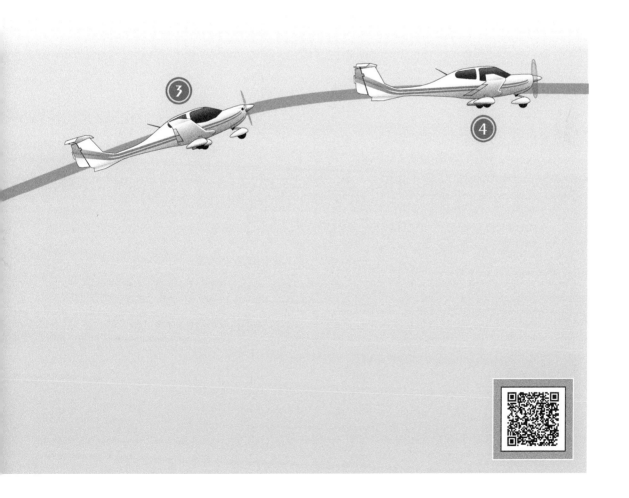

8 — Descents

The descent is a basic flight maneuver to lose altitude without gaining excessive airspeed. You control the rate of descent with pitch attitude and, in some cases, power. You will practice descents at cruise airspeed and at the airspeed used for approaches to landings, including a power-off glide. You must know the power settings, pitch attitudes, and flight instrument indications for each type of descent.

Refer to the AFM/POH for the specific airspeed corresponding to the type of descent you want to perform. When you perform a descent, establish the proper flight attitude using outside references first, then cross-check the attitude using the flight instruments.

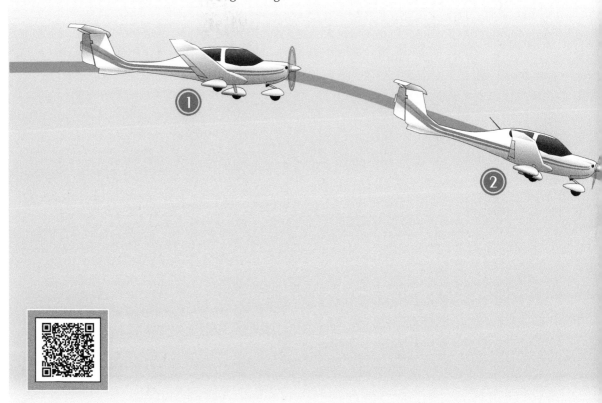

 Establish the descent attitude. After clearing the airspace around the airplane, apply carburetor heat (if applicable) and reduce power as required. Gradually apply back pressure to maintain altitude while the airplane slows to the descent airspeed. When you reach the descent airspeed, lower the nose slightly to set the descent pitch attitude and maintain airspeed. Trim to relieve control pressures.

> In many airplanes, the descent attitude is nearly the same as that used for straight-and-level cruising flight. Although you normally control a descent with power and/or pitch attitude changes, you can also use configuration changes. Extending the landing gear (if applicable) or flaps increases the descent rate without increasing airspeed.

 Maintain the descent attitude and heading. Adjust pitch and power to maintain the descent rate and desired airspeed. Cross check the nose position in relation to the horizon with the airspeed indicator, the vertical speed indicator, and the pitch attitude on the attitude indicator to ensure you are maintaining the correct airspeed and rate of descent.

- In a power-off glide, pitch attitude controls airspeed; raise the nose to decrease airspeed, and lower the nose to increase airspeed. Always trim after you adjust the pitch.

> You might use a power-off glide during a normal approach and landing or in an emergency. In either situation, your workload is high so you might easily be distracted and let the airspeed get too low or too high if you do not properly trim the airplane.

- To maintain a constant airspeed in a powered descent, adjust the pitch attitude when you change power. Increase the pitch attitude slightly when adding power and decrease the pitch attitude when reducing power. Always trim after you adjust pitch or power.

A stabilized approach is essential to landing proficiency. Therefore, to prepare for approach and landings, pitch at a constant attitude and let the airspeed stabilize at approach speed, making small pitch and power changes to maintain the proper attitude and airspeed. Do not make large power adjustments or rapidly and frequently change pitch.

- To maintain heading, refer to the position of each wingtip in relation to the horizon and cross check using the heading indicator. Also, check the turn coordinator to ensure you maintain coordinated flight. If changes are necessary, make small adjustments, allow the airplane to stabilize again, and then trim to relieve control pressures.

MANEUVER 8 ■ **Descents**

③ Begin leveling off at the appropriate point. If you are descending at 500 ft/min, return to straight-and-level flight by gradually raising the nose approximately 50 feet prior to the desired leveloff altitude. Add power to maintain airspeed

Generally, a 10% lead is sufficient for leveloff. For example, 10% of a 500 ft/min climb would yield a 50-foot lead for leveloff.

④ Return to cruise flight. After the airplane is stabilized in straight-and-level cruising flight, set the carburetor heat to COLD (if applicable) and adjust the power to the cruise setting. Enrichen the mixture (if necessary), and trim to relieve control pressures.

Descents

The *Private Pilot Airman Certification Standards (ACS)* do not include specific criteria for descents using outside references. However, you can refer to the performance standards for constant-airspeed descents solely by reference to instruments. See Maneuver 30 — Attitude Instrument Flying.

9 — Turns

You turn the airplane by banking the wings in the desired direction of the turn. Lift is divided into both vertical and horizontal lift components as a result of the bank. The horizontal component of lift moves the airplane toward the banked direction. You normally begin by practicing level turns and, once mastered, move on to climbing and descending turns. Turns are divided into three classes:

- **Shallow turn**—less than approximately 20° angle of bank.
- **Medium turn**—between approximately 20° to 45° angle of bank.
- **Steep turn**—approximately 45° angle of bank or more.

LEVEL TURNS

When you turn by using outside references, the nose of the airplane appears to move in an arc with respect to the horizon. You can determine when you have reached the proper angle of bank by observing the angle of the cowling and instrument panel with respect to the horizon.

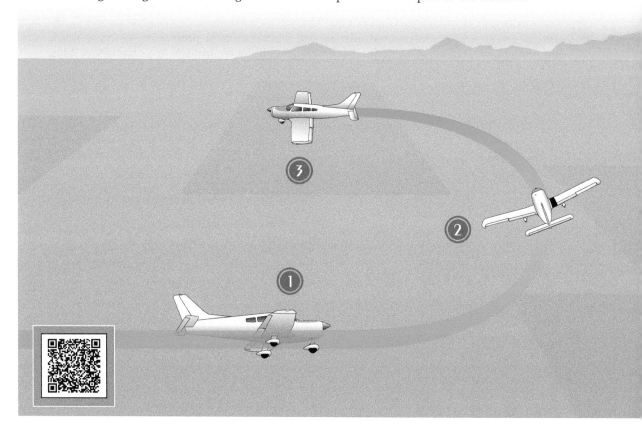

Roll into the turn. After clearing the airspace around the airplane, add power slightly, and move the control wheel in the direction you want to turn. Apply rudder pressure in the direction of the turn. Add back pressure on the control wheel to maintain altitude.

> The ailerons control the roll rate, as well as the angle of bank. The rate at which the airplane rolls depends on how much aileron deflection you use. How far the airplane rolls (steepness of the bank) depends on how long you deflect the ailerons because the airplane continues to roll as long as the ailerons are deflected.

 Maintain a coordinated turn. When you reach the desired angle of bank, neutralize the ailerons. Use the rudder to maintain coordinated flight. Maintain the correct bank and pitch attitude using outside references and cross checking with the instruments. Trim to relieve control pressures.

> Do not attempt to perform the turn solely by instrument reference.
>
> A flat skidding turn occurs if you hold excessive rudder in the direction of the turn to avoid banking the airplane. Be alert for both slips and skids in the turn.

 Roll out of the turn at the appropriate lead point. Lead the roll-out by approximately 1/2 of the bank angle. Use coordinated aileron and rudder control pressures as you roll out. Simultaneously, begin releasing the back pressure on the control wheel so aileron, rudder, and elevator/stabilator pressures are neutralized when the airplane reaches the wings-level position. Upon reaching a wings-level attitude, reduce power and trim to relieve control pressures.

> Leading your roll-out heading by 1/2 your bank angle is a good rule of thumb for initial training. However, keep in mind that the required amount of lead depends on the type of turn, turn rate, and rollout rate. As you gain experience, you will develop a consistent roll-in and roll-out technique for various types of turns.

MANEUVER 9 ▪ **Turns**

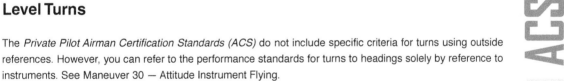

Level Turns

The *Private Pilot Airman Certification Standards (ACS)* do not include specific criteria for turns using outside references. However, you can refer to the performance standards for turns to headings solely by reference to instruments. See Maneuver 30 — Attitude Instrument Flying.

CLIMBING TURNS

The objective of practicing climbing turns is to smoothly combine the techniques of climbs with those of turns. Initially, you might practice climbing turns with a two-step process. First, you establish climb power and attitude and then roll to the desired angle of bank. As you gain experience and proficiency, you will enter the maneuver by establishing both the climb and bank attitude at the same time.

Although you maintain the same airspeed in climbing turns as in straight climbs, your rate of climb is less for climbing turns because the vertical lift component is less when the airplane banks. Generally, you perform climbing turns using shallow bank angles, because steep bank angles divert more of the vertical component of lift, which reduces the rate of climb.

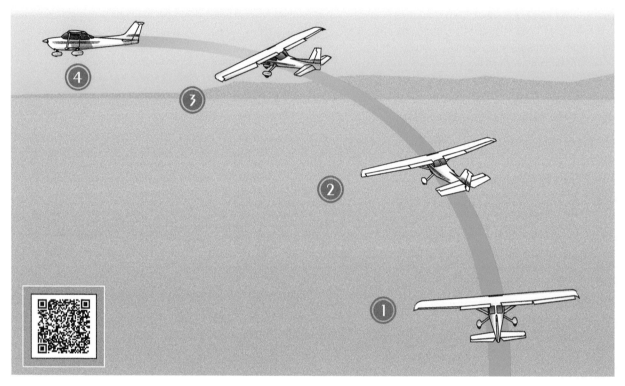

1. **Roll into the turn and begin the climb.** After clearing the airspace around the airplane, simultaneously add power, apply back pressure on the control wheel and turn the airplane in the desired direction with coordinated aileron and rudder control input.

2. **Maintain the turn and climb.** When you reach the desired angle of bank, neutralize the ailerons. Trim to relieve control pressures. Maintain the desired climb airspeed and angle of bank using outside references, periodically cross checking the flight instruments.

3. **Roll out of the turn and level off from the climb.** Lead the roll-out by approximately 1/2 of the bank angle. Use coordinated aileron and rudder control pressures as you roll out. Simultaneously, begin releasing the back pressure on the control wheel so aileron, rudder, and elevator/stabilator pressures are neutralized when the airplane reaches the desired heading and altitude.

> You rarely reach the desired altitude and heading at the same time. If you reach the heading first, level the wings and maintain the climb until you reach the desired altitude. If you reach the altitude first, lower the nose to maintain the desired altitude and continue the turn toward the desired heading. If you reach both the desired altitude and heading at the same time, you can perform these procedures simultaneously.

④ **Return to cruise flight.** When the airplane reaches the desired cruise airspeed, reduce power, trim to relieve control pressures, and lean the mixture (if necessary).

Climbing Turns

The *Private Pilot Airman Certification Standards (ACS)* do not include specific criteria for climbing turns using outside references. However, you can refer to the performance standards for constant-airspeed climbs and turns to headings solely by reference to instruments. See Maneuver 30 — Attitude Instrument Flying.

DESCENDING TURNS

Descending turns to preselected headings and altitudes combine the procedures for straight descents with those used in turns. As with climbing turns, you might practice descending turns using a two-step process. First, you establish the descent attitude, then roll to the desired angle of bank. As you gain proficiency, you will learn to establish the descent attitude and bank simultaneously.

Although you maintain the same airspeed in descending turns as in straight descents, your rate of descent is higher in a descending turn with a comparable power setting because the vertical lift component is less when the airplane banks. You can compensate for this with a slight addition of power over what is used in a straight descent.

MANEUVER 9 ■ **Turns**

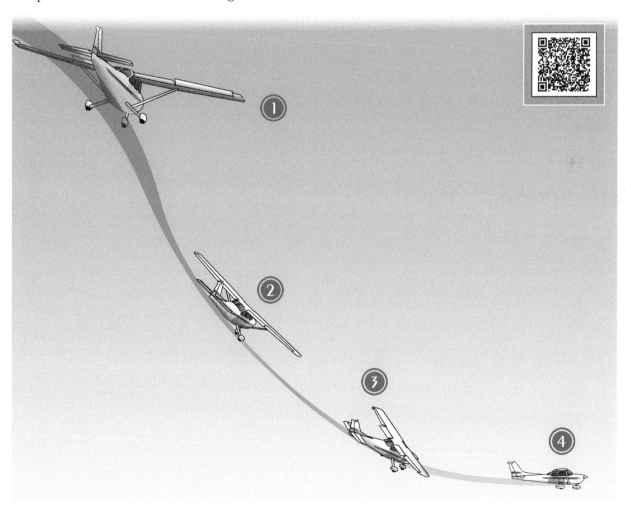

Roll into the turn and begin the descent. After clearing the airspace around the airplane, apply carburetor heat (if applicable), reduce power, and lower the nose. Simultaneously, turn toward the desired heading using coordinated aileron and rudder application.

Maintain the turn and descent. When you reach the desired angle of bank, neutralize the ailerons. Maintain the desired descent airspeed and angle of bank using outside references, periodically cross checking your flight instruments. Trim to relieve control pressures.

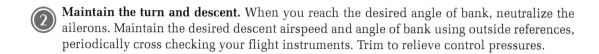

Use power to control the rate of descent. Make the initial power setting for the desired rate of descent and allow the pitch attitude and the rate of descent to stabilize. If you desire a higher rate of descent, reduce power. In contrast, add power if you desire a lower rate of descent.

Roll out of the turn and level off from the descent. Lead the roll-out by approximately 1/2 of the bank angle. Use coordinated aileron and rudder control pressures as you roll out. Simultaneously, add power to the cruise setting and adjust the nose position so aileron, rudder, and elevator/stabilator pressures are neutralized when the airplane reaches the desired heading and altitude.

Return to cruise flight. Set the carburetor heat to COLD (if applicable), trim to relieve control pressures, and, if necessary, enrichen the mixture.

MANEUVER 9 ■ Turns

Descending Turns

The *Private Pilot Airman Certification Standards (ACS)* do not include specific criteria for descending turns using outside references. However, you can refer to the performance standards for constant-airspeed descents and turns to headings solely by reference to instruments. See Maneuver 30 — Attitude Instrument Flying.

EXERCISES — BASIC MANEUVERS

6 — STRAIGHT-AND-LEVEL FLIGHT

1. During straight-and-level flight, what primary visual reference do you use for maintaining altitude and heading?

_____

2. What is a safety-related advantage of focusing outside the flight deck?

_____

3. True/False. To maintain straight-and-level flight, you normally need to make a continuous series of small adjustments in pitch and bank.

4. What is the primary reason for adjusting the trim?
   A. To correct heading
   B. To change pitch attitude
   C. To relieve control pressures

5. How can you determine the magnitude of a deviation from your desired heading and altitude?

_____

7 — CLIMBS

1. Which climb speed provides the greatest gain in altitude in the shortest distance?

_____

2. Which climb speed provides the most gain in altitude in the least amount of time?

_____

3. True/False. As the pitch attitude is increased and the airspeed decreases, left-turning tendencies become less pronounced.

4. Would you expect a need for a decrease or increase of right rudder pressure as the airplane accelerates during leveloff?

_____

5. What percentage of your vertical speed should you normally use to determine the lead for leveloff? _____

MANEUVER 9 ▪ **Turns**

8 — DESCENTS

1. True/False. You can control your rate of descent with pitch attitude.

2. Does a cruise descent result in a higher or lower groundspeed than a typical descent used for approach to landing?

   _____

3. During a 500 ft/min descent, you have been instructed to level off at 4,000 feet. At what altitude should you begin your leveloff?

   _____

4. True/False. You can increase your descent rate by lowering the flaps.

5. Would increasing the power during a constant airspeed, power-on descent require you to raise or lower the nose to maintain airspeed?

   _____

9 — TURNS

1. What are the three classes of turns and how many degrees of bank are associated with each?

   _____

2. True/False. During a level turn, you maintain the same amount of aileron deflection throughout the turn.

3. What determines the roll rate?

   _____

4. You are in a climbing turn to the right, using a 30° angle of bank, and have been directed to rollout on a heading of 090°. On what heading should you begin your rollout?_____

5. How can you compensate for the increased rate of descent you experience in a descending turn, as opposed to a straight descent?

   _____

CHAPTER 3

Airport Operations

10 — Normal Takeoff and Climb

Each takeoff is affected by the wind conditions, runway surface and length, and possible obstructions at the end of the runway. The takeoff procedures outlined here are provided as general guidelines only. Be sure to consult your airplane's AFM/POH for the proper checklists and procedures.

 Prepare for the takeoff. Complete the before takeoff check, which includes following the Before Takeoff checklist to verify the operation of systems and equipment and performing the takeoff briefing to review takeoff performance and procedures. Ensure that the runway, as well as the approach and departure paths are clear of other aircraft.

- At an uncontrolled airport, broadcast your intentions for departure on the common traffic advisory frequency (CTAF).

- At a controlled airport, contact the tower and inform the controller you are ready for departure. You must obtain a clearance from the control tower prior to taxiing onto the runway, and prior to takeoff.

> Select the takeoff runway based on your capability, the airplane performance and limitations, available distance, and wind. If you are uncomfortable with runway conditions, such as a strong crosswind or short distance, you might be able to request another runway at a controlled airport.

 Taxi onto the runway. Ensure that the runway and the approach and departure paths are clear of other aircraft. Line up with the runway centerline, center the nosewheel, and neutralize the ailerons. Check the windsock to determine the wind position in relation to the runway and then begin the takeoff roll.

 Add takeoff power.

- Advance the throttle smoothly to takeoff power, and as the airplane starts to roll, select a point on the cowling through which the centerline of the runway passes and use it as a reference point for directional control. Apply right rudder to counteract engine torque.

> Abruptly applying power can cause the airplane to yaw sharply to the left due to the torque effects of the engine and propeller.

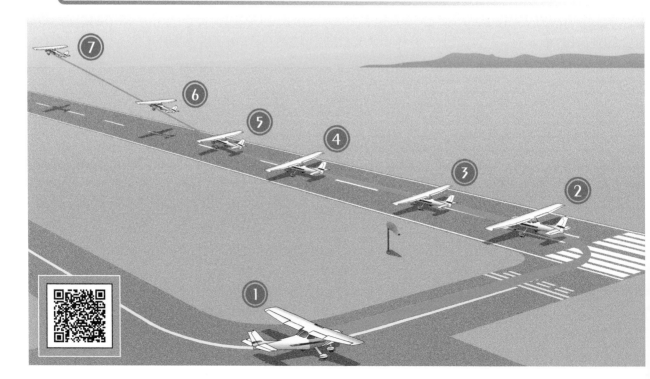

- Check the engine instruments to ensure the engine is developing full power and is functioning within its operational limits. Slow acceleration or any hesitation in power is sufficient reason to abort the takeoff.

> Keep your hand on the throttle throughout the takeoff to ensure that the throttle does not slide back during the takeoff roll. You will also be able to reduce power to idle quickly if you decide to reject the takeoff.

- Maintain directional control with the rudder pedals and use a neutral aileron position if the wind is aligned with the runway.

> So you do not press the brakes inadvertently, rest your feet on the floor with the balls of your feet on the bottom edges of the rudder pedals.

 Adjust control pressures as the airplane accelerates. As the controls become effective, reduce rudder pressure to maintain directional control and apply slight back pressure to the control wheel.

 Establish the takeoff attitude to lift the airplane off the runway. Add back pressure on the control wheel at the speed recommended in the AFM/POH. As the airplane lifts off the runway, note the nose position in relation to the horizon and then maintain this attitude by using elevator/stabilator pressure.

> The takeoff attitude is a compromise between holding the nose on the ground and selecting an attitude that is too nose high. If you hold the nosewheel on the ground too long, the airplane tends to build excess airspeed, which increases the takeoff distance. Holding an excessively nose-high attitude can force the airplane into the air prematurely and then cause it to settle back to the runway. Also, the airplane might be at such a high angle of attack (high drag condition) that it cannot accelerate to climb speed.

 Establish the climb attitude. Accelerate to the climb speed recommended by the AFM/POH and adjust the pitch attitude to maintain the climb speed. Fly the departure leg of the traffic pattern straight out on an extension of the runway centerline. Use right rudder to counteract the airplane's left-turning tendency.

> The initial climb speed varies with the airplane flap position and local conditions, such as the presence of obstacles in the departure path. You might need to fly at the obstacle clearance speed, best angle-of-climb speed (V_X), or best rate-of-climb speed(V_Y), as specified in the AFM/POH.

 Stabilize the climb. After reaching a safe altitude, adjust the power to the recommended climb setting and trim to relieve control pressures. Complete the Climb checklist in the AFM/POH, and depart or remain in the traffic pattern.

> If a control tower is in operation, you can request and usually receive approval for any type of departure. The standard procedure for departing an uncontrolled airport is to fly straight out or to make a 45° turn in the direction of the traffic pattern.
>
> Ensure you know and comply with any noise abatement procedures after takeoff.

MANEUVER 10 ■ **Normal Takeoff and Climb**

REJECTED TAKEOFF

Although rare, you might encounter an emergency or abnormal situation that requires you to reject the takeoff while still on the runway. Reasons to reject a takeoff include:

- A hazard on the runway.

- A loss of power.

- An engine or equipment malfunction.

- A loss of directional control.

- An uncomfortable feeling about how the takeoff is progressing.

Before takeoff, identify a point along the runway at which the airplane should be airborne based on your knowledge of the airplane performance under the existing conditions. If you reach that point and the airplane is not airborne, reject the takeoff by reducing the power to idle, maintaining directional control with the rudder pedals, and applying brakes. In addition, if you begin to lose directional control of the airplane, immediately reject the takeoff to prevent the airplane from exiting the runway. If you properly plan and perform a rejected takeoff, you should be able to stop the airplane on the remaining runway without using extraordinary measures, such as excessive braking.

ENGINE FAILURE DURING TAKEOFF

Although an engine malfunction on takeoff is rare, the possibility does exist. If you experience a power loss on the takeoff roll, reject the takeoff immediately. If the engine malfunction occurs just after liftoff, you should reduce the pitch attitude slightly and allow the airplane to settle back to the runway. If sufficient runway does not exist, and you have not yet attained a safe maneuvering altitude, you must land straight ahead. In this situation, you should make only small heading changes to avoid obstacles and should not attempt to turn back to the runway. Refer to Maneuver 17 — Emergency Approach and Landing for the step-by-step procedure to manage an engine failure after takeoff.

IV. **Takeoffs, Landings, and Go-Arounds**

Task	A. Normal Takeoff and Climb
References	FAA-H-8083-2, FAA-H-8083-3, FAA-H-8083-23; POH/AFM; AIM
Objective	To determine that the applicant exhibits satisfactory knowledge, risk management, and skills associated with a normal takeoff, climb operations, and rejected takeoff procedures. ***Note:*** *If a crosswind condition does not exist, the applicant's knowledge of crosswind elements must be evaluated through oral testing.*
Knowledge	The applicant demonstrates understanding of:
PA.IV.A.K1	Effects of atmospheric conditions, including wind, on takeoff and climb performance.
PA.IV.A.K2	V_X and V_Y.
PA.IV.A.K3	Appropriate airplane configuration.
Risk Management	The applicant demonstrates the ability to identify, assess and mitigate risks, encompassing:
PA.IV.A.R1	Selection of runway based on pilot capability, airplane performance and limitations, available distance, and wind.
PA.IV.A.R2	Effects of:
PA.IV.A.R2a	a. Crosswind
PA.IV.A.R2b	b. Windshear
PA.IV.A.R2c	c. Tailwind
PA.IV.A.R2d	d. Wake turbulence
PA.IV.A.R2e	e. Runway surface/condition
PA.IV.A.R3	Abnormal operations, to include planning for:
PA.IV.A.R3a	a. Rejected takeoff
PA.IV.A.R3b	b. Engine failure in takeoff/climb phase of flight
PA.IV.A.R4	Collision hazards, to include aircraft, vehicles, vessels, persons, wildlife, terrain, obstacles, and wires.
PA.IV.A.R5	Low altitude maneuvering including stall, spin, or CFIT.
PA.IV.A.R6	Distractions, loss of situational awareness, and/or improper task management.
Skills	The applicant demonstrates the ability to:
PA.IV.A.S1	Complete the appropriate checklist.
PA.IV.A.S2	Make radio calls as appropriate.
PA.IV.A.S3	Verify assigned/correct runway.
PA.IV.A.S4	Ascertain wind direction with or without visible wind direction indicators.
PA.IV.A.S5	Position the flight controls for the existing wind conditions.
PA.IV.A.S6	Clear the area; taxi into takeoff position and align the airplane on the runway centerline (ASEL, AMEL) or takeoff path (ASES, AMES).
PA.IV.A.S7	Confirm takeoff power and proper engine and flight instrument indications prior to rotation (ASEL, AMEL).
PA.IV.A.S8	Rotate and lift off at the recommended airspeed and accelerate to V_Y.
PA.IV.A.S9	Retract the water rudders, as appropriate, establish and maintain the most efficient planing/liftoff attitude, and correct for porpoising and skipping (ASES, AMES).
PA.IV.A.S10	Establish a pitch attitude to maintain the manufacturer's recommended speed or V_Y, +10/-5 knots.
PA.IV.A.S11	Configure the airplane in accordance with manufacturer's guidance.
PA.IV.A.S12	Maintain V_Y +10/-5 knots to a safe maneuvering altitude.
PA.IV.A.S13	Maintain directional control and proper wind-drift correction throughout takeoff and climb.
PA.IV.A.S14	Comply with noise abatement procedures.

MANEUVER 10 ■ **Normal Takeoff and Climb**

11 — Crosswind Takeoff and Climb

A crosswind takeoff is much like a normal takeoff, except you have to use the flight controls to counteract the crosswind component. The term crosswind component refers to that part of the wind that acts at a right angle to the airplane's path on takeoff or landing. You can calculate this component with a crosswind component chart or with a flight computer.

To perform takeoffs with strong crosswinds, follow the guidelines for flap settings in the AFM/POH. You typically use the minimum flap setting necessary for the field length to reduce the drift angle immediately after takeoff. The AFM/POH normally lists a maximum demonstrated crosswind velocity for takeoff and landing. Base your personal crosswind limit on your skill level and any limitation specified by your instructor. In addition, flight training operators often have specified limits based on pilot experience and/or proficiency. The following step-by-step procedure does not cover every aspect of a takeoff but emphasizes procedures specific to crosswind takeoffs.

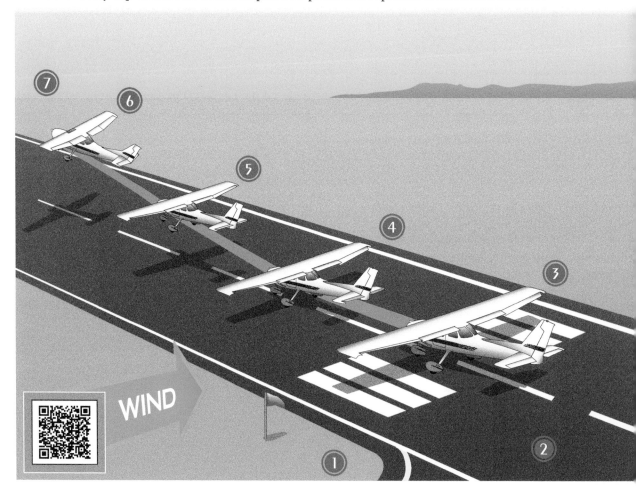

WIND

① **Prepare for the takeoff.** Complete the before takeoff check. Ensure you include the wind direction and speed and a review of crosswind takeoff procedures in your takeoff briefing.

② **Taxi onto the runway.** After obtaining a clearance (at a controlled airport) or self announcing your intentions (at an uncontrolled airport), taxi onto the runway and line up with the runway centerline. Center the nosewheel and fully turn the control wheel in the direction of the wind, placing the upwind aileron in the up position. For example, if the crosswind is blowing from your left, fully move the control stick to the left, placing the left aileron in the up position. This control deflection compensates for the crosswind's tendency to push and roll the airplane to the downwind side of the runway.

Add takeoff power. Check the engine indications to verify the engine is developing full power and operating within its limits. Maintain aileron deflection into the wind. Use rudder pressure to counteract engine torque and the airplane's weathervaning tendency.

> Apply downwind rudder pressure to prevent the airplane from weathervaning into the wind. When you increase power for takeoff, torque and P-factor cause the airplane to yaw to the left. This yaw might be sufficient to counteract the airplane's tendency to weathervane into the wind in a crosswind from the right. However, this left-turning tendency can aggravate weathervaning in a crosswind from the left.

 Adjust the control pressures as the airplane accelerates. As the airplane accelerates and the controls become more effective, reduce the aileron deflection gradually so it is just sufficient to counteract the rolling tendency. Reduce rudder pressure as necessary.

> The amount of aileron and rudder deflection required to compensate for a crosswind during the takeoff roll depends on the crosswind component. When you use the right amount of crosswind correction, the airplane tracks straight down the runway and you feel no side load on the landing gear.
>
> Aileron pressure throughout the takeoff roll keeps the crosswind from raising the upwind wing. If the upwind wing rises, the amount of wing surface exposed to the crosswind increases, which can cause side-skipping. These sideways bounces can stress the landing gear and can cause structural failure.

⑤ Establish the takeoff attitude to lift the airplane off the runway. For a greater airspeed on liftoff with increased control capabilities, hold the airplane on the runway until you attain a slightly higher-than-normal liftoff speed. This technique also reduces the chance of the airplane being lifted off prematurely by a sudden gust of wind.

⑥ Establish the climb attitude. Accelerate to the initial climb speed in the AFM/POH and adjust the pitch attitude to maintain that airspeed. To track straight out on an imaginary extension of the runway centerline, enter a crab—turn the nose into the wind to offset the crosswind, level the wings, and adjust the rudder pressure to maintain runway alignment.

⑦ Stabilize the climb. After you reach a safe altitude, adjust the power to the recommended climb setting and trim the aircraft to relieve any control pressures. Complete the Climb checklist and depart or remain in the traffic pattern.

> If a control tower is in operation, you can request and usually receive approval for any type of departure. The standard procedure for departing an uncontrolled airport is to fly straight-out or to make a 45° turn in the direction of the traffic pattern.

The Private Pilot Airman Certification Standards (ACS) for the Normal Takeoff and Climb task also apply to a crosswind takeoff and climb. See page 3-5.

MANEUVER 11 ■ Crosswind Takeoff and Climb

12 — Traffic Patterns

Standard traffic patterns are used to improve both the safety and efficiency of airport operations and are particularly important at airports without operating control towers. The standard traffic pattern is rectangular and has five named legs; downwind, base, final, departure, and crosswind. The direction of the pattern refers to the orientation of the pattern turns. For example, aircraft in a left-hand traffic pattern make left turns to base, final, crosswind, and downwind. Normally, a left-hand pattern is used to give the left-seat pilot the best view of the runway and the surrounding environment.

In some cases, a right-hand traffic pattern might be used to avoid obstacles, terrain, restricted airspace, noise sensitive areas, or other runways. Both left-hand and right-hand traffic patterns normally are used when simultaneous operations are conducted on parallel runways. Other special considerations can require additional variations to the standard traffic pattern. You can find information regarding specific airport traffic patterns in flight informations sources, such as the applicable Chart Supplement, *Aeronautical Information Manual (AIM), FAR Part 93,* and Notices to Airmen (NOTAMs).

CONTROLLED AND UNCONTROLLED AIRPORTS

At airports with operating control towers (controlled airports), you are required by regulations to establish and maintain radio communication with the tower. When you fly at a controlled airport, you typically listen to the automatic terminal information service (ATIS) to obtain airport advisory information before contacting the tower. The tower controller provides instructions for you to enter the traffic pattern at a specific position and to report that position. After you enter the traffic pattern, the tower controller clears you to land when appropriate. If you are taking off and remaining in

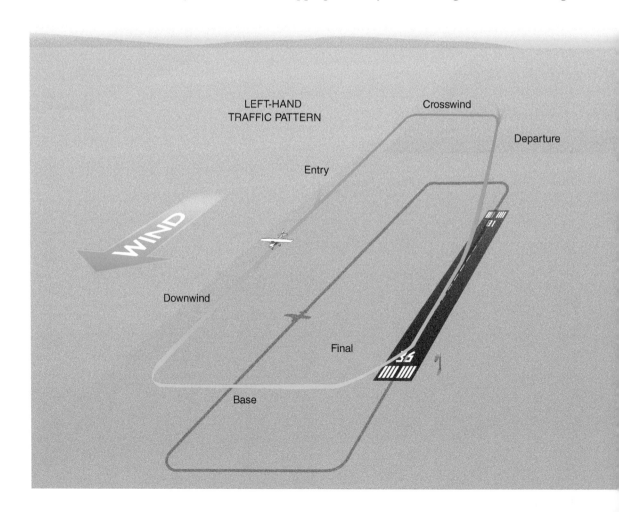

the traffic pattern, the controller provides instructions to enter a left- or right-hand pattern for a particular runway and might direct you to follow another aircraft in the pattern.

At airports without control towers (uncontrolled airports), you are not required to have or use a radio. However, if your airplane is radio equipped while operating within 10 miles of any airport, you should monitor and communicate on the common traffic advisory frequency (CTAF). The CTAF may be a UNICOM, MULTICOM or tower frequency. At some airports in Alaska with a flight service station (FSS) on the field, the CTAF is an FSS frequency (normally 123.6). Before transmitting on the CTAF, monitor the frequency for a short time to visualize the traffic situation and plan for entering the pattern. Report your airplane identification, position, and intentions. Include the name of the airport at the beginning and end of each broadcast, because more than one airport can be assigned the same frequency.

If you are unfamiliar with the airport and cannot obtain information from a UNICOM operator, control tower, or automated weather station, overfly the airport at least 500 feet above the traffic pattern altitude to determine the landing runway and the associated pattern direction. Use visual indicators such as the segmented circle, wind direction indicator, landing direction indicator, or traffic pattern indicator. An example of a radio call for an aircraft conducting an overflight of the airport to determine the landing information is: *"Coronado traffic, Cessna 23455, 10 miles south descending through 4,000, overflying for landing, Coronado."*

FLYING THE TRAFFIC PATTERN

The basic procedures for flying the legs of the traffic pattern are the same regardless of whether you are operating at a controlled or uncontrolled airport. The following steps cover the procedures and radio calls for flying each leg of the traffic pattern using an example of entering the traffic pattern at an uncontrolled airport while in flight.

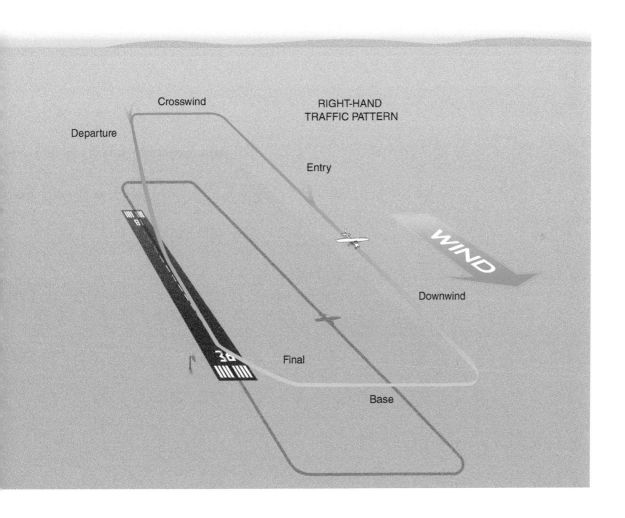

Traffic Patterns

MANEUVER 12

① **Obtain airport information.** Review your chart and set radio frequencies. Then listen to an automated weather reporting station or contact the UNICOM operator for an airport advisory. *"Coronado UNICOM, Cessna 23455, 15 miles northeast descending through 4,000, landing Coronado, request wind and traffic information, Coronado."*

② **Prepare for pattern entry.** Visualize the pattern entry, complete the before landing briefing and begin the Before Landing checklist, Broadcast your intentions on the CTAF. State your intentions on the CTAF at least 10 miles from the airport, *"Coronado traffic, 10 miles northeast, will be entering a midfield left downwind for Runway 9, Coronado."*

> Although you can begin the Before Landing checklist to accomplish certain tasks, such as turning on the landing light, you will defer other tasks, such as flap extension, until you are in traffic pattern.

③ **Enter the traffic pattern.** Use a 45° angle to the downwind leg, abeam the midpoint of the runway, at pattern altitude (normally 1,000 feet AGL). *"Coronado traffic, Cessna 23455, entering downwind for Runway 9, touch-and-go, Coronado."*

> Establish the airplane at pattern altitude while well clear of the pattern prior to entry.

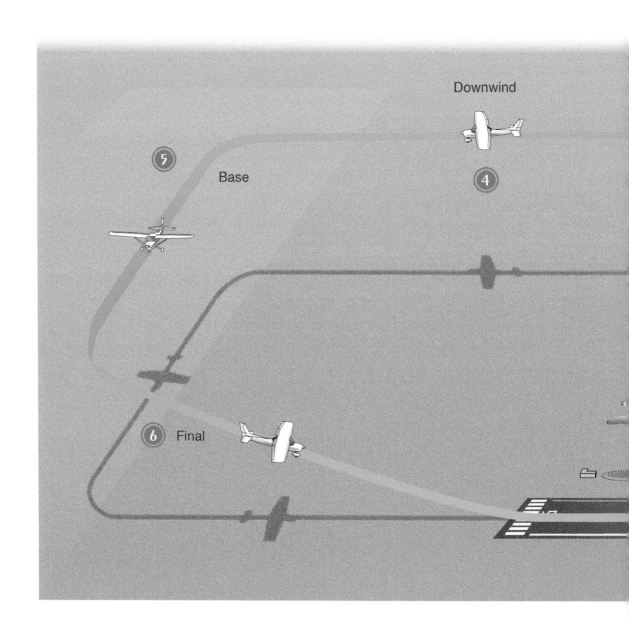

Fly the downwind leg. Fly parallel to the runway. Maintain pattern altitude until abeam the intended landing point, then begin your descent for landing.

> You might have to delay the start of your descent to follow other traffic in the pattern.

 Turn onto the base leg. Begin your turn when the touchdown point is approximately 45° behind the inside wingtip. *"Coronado traffic Cessna 23455, base, Runway 9, touch-and-go, Coronado."*

> Turn to base using approximately 30° angle of bank. Adjust the base leg to follow other traffic and compensate for the prevailing wind conditions. For example, with a strong tailwind you will need to begin your turn to base leg sooner than normal so that you do not drift too far downwind during the turn.

 Turn to final. Begin the final leg at least 1/4 of a mile from the approach end of the runway. Stay aligned with the runway centerline, compensating for crosswind conditions as needed. *"Coronado traffic, Cessna 23455, final, Runway 9, touch and go, Coronado."*

> Your turn to final should be accomplished by using between 20° and 30° angle of bank. Complete the turn at a safe altitude above the terrain, obstructions, and the airport elevation. When approaching a set of parallel runways, you must avoid overshooting the final approach and interfering with the parallel runway traffic.

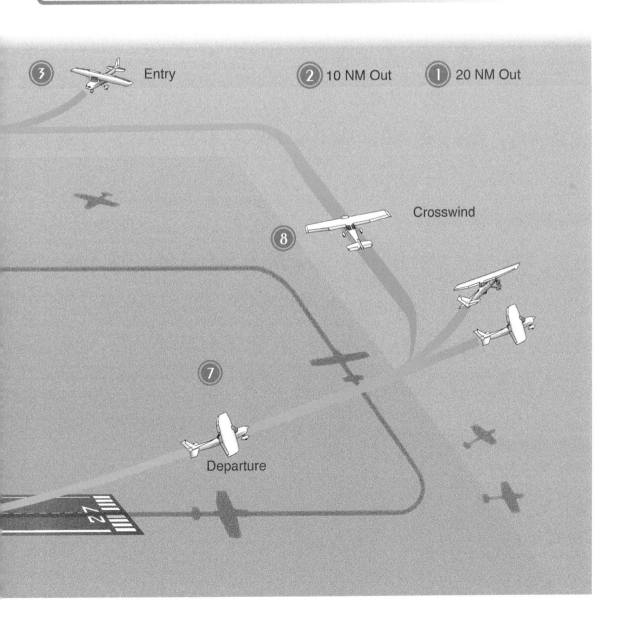

MANEUVER 12 ■ **Traffic Patterns**

Climb out on the departure leg. Stay aligned with the extended runway centerline until you are beyond the departure end of the runway and continue climbing.

> If you are familiar with the airport, you can use ground checkpoints to ensure you maintain a track that corresponds to the runway extended centerline; a crosswind can cause the airplane to drift off the extended centerline even though you maintain runway heading. If traffic causes you to extend your departure, be sure to level off at pattern altitude.

 Depart or remain in the pattern. If you are departing the traffic pattern, continue your climb to pattern altitude, then fly straight out, or exit with a 45° turn to the pattern side of the runway. In either case, comply with the departure procedures established for that airport. *"Coronado traffic, Cessna 23455, departing Runway 9, departing the traffic pattern to the northeast, climbing to 5,500, Coronado."*

If you are remaining in the traffic pattern, climb on the departure leg to within 300 feet of pattern altitude before turning on the crosswind leg. Continue your climb to pattern altitude on the crosswind leg. After reaching pattern altitude, level off and continue to fly 90° to the runway until you are ready to turn downwind.

> If you are departing from one of a set of parallel runways, ensure your ground track does not penetrate the departure path of the other runway(s). Unless regulations or local procedures dictate otherwise, you should monitor/communicate on the CTAF until 10 miles from the airport.
>
> If you are remaining in the pattern, check for other traffic in the pattern before starting your turn to crosswind. If necessary, extend your departure leg to follow other aircraft.

COLLISION AVOIDANCE

Because most collisions occur near airports, traffic pattern operations require a continuous effort to see and avoid other aircraft. Use these collision avoidance procedures at both controlled and uncontrolled airports:

- Always check both the approach and departure ends of a runway prior to takeoff or landing.

- Turn on anticollision and landing lights in the traffic pattern and within a 10-mile radius of the airport.

- When departing, accelerate to cruise climb airspeed as soon as practical.

- Prior to all turns, check for traffic.

- Monitor the appropriate radio frequency and listen for information concerning other air traffic.

RUNWAY INCURSION AVOIDANCE

Runway incursions usually are caused by errors associated with clearances, communications, airport surface movement, and positional awareness. Take these actions to help prevent a runway incursion while you are operating in the traffic pattern:

- Read back (in full) all clearances involving runway crossing, hold short, or line up and wait instructions.

- Maintain a sterile cockpit while in the traffic pattern, do not become absorbed in unnecessary conversation.

- While in a runup area or waiting for a clearance, position your airplane so that you can see landing aircraft.

- Monitor radio frequencies for information about other aircraft cleared onto your runway for takeoff or landing. Be alert for aircraft on other frequencies or without radio communication.

- After landing, stay on the tower frequency until instructed to change frequencies.

- Use your exterior taxi/landing lights when practical to help others see your airplane (especially during periods of reduced visibility or at night).

- Make sure you understand the required procedures if you fly into or out of an airport where land and hold short operations (LAHSO) are in effect.

WAKE TURBULENCE

When an airplane generates lift, air spills over the wingtips from the high pressure areas below the wings to the low pressure areas above them, causing rapidly rotating whirlpools of air called wingtip vortices, or wake turbulence. The greatest wake turbulence is produced by large, heavy aircraft operating at low speeds, high angles of attack, and in a clean configuration. Because these conditions are most closely duplicated on takeoff and landing, be alert for wake turbulence near airports used by large airplanes. Avoid the area below and behind large aircraft to avoid dangerous wingtip vortices that can upset your aircraft. Refer to the *Aeronautical Information Manual (AIM)* and the Jeppesen *Private Pilot* textbook for wake turbulence avoidance procedures.

WIND SHEAR

Wind shear is a sudden, drastic shift in wind speed and/or direction that can occur at any altitude in a vertical or horizontal plane. Wind shear can subject your airplane to sudden updrafts, downdrafts, or extreme horizontal wind components, causing loss of lift or violent changes in vertical speeds or altitudes. Ensure that you know the conditions favorable for wind shear and that you are aware of any wind shear reports and forecasts. Anticipate wind shear when frontal systems and thunderstorms are in the area. To help detect hazardous wind shear associated with microbursts, low-level wind shear alert systems (LLWAS) are installed at many airports. If you are arriving or departing from an airport equipped with LLWAS, ATC will advise if an alert is posted and will provided wind velocities at two or more of the sensors.

MANEUVER 12 ▪ Traffic Patterns

III. Airport and Seaplane Base Operations

Task	B. Traffic Patterns
References	14 CFR part 91; FAA-H-8083-2, FAA-H-8083-25; AIM
Objective	To determine that the applicant exhibits satisfactory knowledge, risk management, and skills associated with traffic patterns.
Knowledge	The applicant demonstrates understanding of:
PA.III.B.K1	Towered and nontowered airport operations.
PA.III.B.K2	Runway selection for the current conditions.
PA.III.B.K3	Right-of-way rules.
PA.III.B.K4	Use of automated weather and airport information.
Risk Management	The applicant demonstrates the ability to identify, assess and mitigate risks, encompassing:
PA.III.B.R1	Collision hazards, to include aircraft, terrain, obstacles, and wires.
PA.III.B.R2	Distractions, loss of situational awareness, and/or improper task management.
PA.III.B.R3	Wake turbulence and/or windshear.
Skills	The applicant demonstrates the ability to:
PA.III.B.S1	Properly identify and interpret airport/seaplane base runways, taxiways, markings, signs, and lighting.
PA.III.B.S2	Comply with recommended traffic pattern procedures.
PA.III.B.S3	Correct for wind drift to maintain the proper ground track.
PA.III.B.S4	Maintain orientation with the runway/landing area in use.
PA.III.B.S5	Maintain traffic pattern altitude, ±100 feet, and the appropriate airspeed, ±10 knots.
PA.III.B.S6	Maintain situational awareness and proper spacing from other aircraft in the traffic pattern.

13 — Normal Approach and Landing

Successfully landing an airplane is probably the most challenging, as well as satisfying, phase of a flight. Although the basic techniques to fly a normal approach and landing apply, every landing is different due to varying wind conditions, runway surface and length, and possible obstructions at the approach end of the runway. In addition, you must consider the effects of wake turbulence and wind shear. For example, you might need to adjust your approach to avoid the wake turbulence from a larger airplane taking off or landing prior to your landing. Refer to Maneuver 12 — Traffic Patterns for more information regarding these hazards.

During approach and landing, you can configure the airplane for landing with no flaps, partial flaps, or full flaps. You typically extend the flaps in increments, which allow you to make smaller adjustments to pitch and power compared to extending full flaps all at one time. Extend the first increment of flaps on the downwind leg and the next on base leg. Usually, you extend full flaps on the final approach leg. Because the full-flap stall speed is less than the no-flap or partial-flap stall speed, landing with full flaps results in a slower touchdown speed and shorter ground roll.

APPROACH

Prior to each landing, complete a before landing briefing and the Before Landing checklist in the AFM/POH. As you fly the traffic pattern at an uncontrolled airport, self-announce your position and/or intentions on the appropriate frequency in accordance with recommended procedures. At a controlled airport, follow the controller's instructions and read back clearances and the runway assignment. Ensure that you are cleared to land prior to touching down on the runway.

(1) Prepare for landing. On the downwind leg, follow the Before Landing checklist to complete each item at the appropriate time and clear the area ahead and to the left and right of your flight path for other traffic. In addition, check for traffic that might be above and descending or below and climbing through your flight path.

> You typically accomplish some of the items on the Before Landing checklist prior to entering the traffic pattern. However, you perform certain tasks, such as extending the flaps or setting the propeller control to high RPM (in an airplane with a constant-speed propeller), in the traffic pattern.

(2) Begin the descent. As you approach the position abeam the intended landing point, you should be at the designated traffic pattern altitude near the airplane's cruising speed.

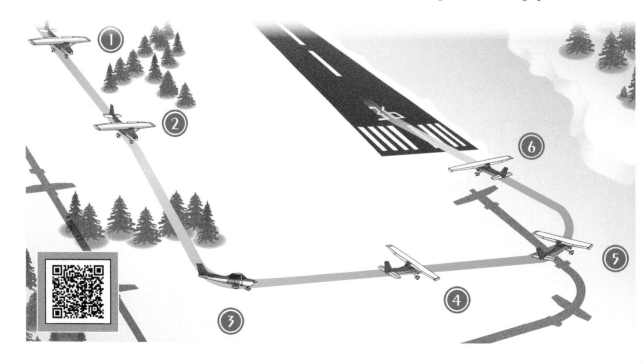

- Reduce the power to the descent power setting while maintaining altitude so that the airplane slows to approach speed.

- Lower the nose to maintain the approach speed in the AFM/POH and initiate a descent.

- Extend the flaps as appropriate.

> You might need to delay the descent if you must extend the downwind leg to follow traffic. Avoid becoming so engrossed with flight deck duties that you are unable to maintain situational awareness.

 Turn onto the base leg. Check for traffic on the base leg and on the extended runway centerline of the final approach. Begin your turn to the base leg after the airplane has descended 100 to 200 feet and the landing point is approximately 45° behind the wing.

> As you turn to base, the wind tends to push the airplane away from the runway. Therefore, you usually need to turn more than 90° to apply the appropriate crab angle.

 Stabilize the approach. Rolling out on base, you are at the key position, an early decision point where you assess and adjust your altitude, airspeed, and distance from the runway to ensure a smooth approach and to avoid large last-minute corrections on short final. Extend flaps as appropriate based on your assessment.

> If the airplane is high at the key position, you should either reduce power, extend additional flaps, or both to avoid landing beyond your desired touchdown point. If the airplane is low or wide on base leg, or if the wind is stronger than normal, you could land short of your desired point. Therefore, you should either begin your turn to final sooner, or add power. Retracting flaps is not considered an acceptable correction.

 Turn to final. Check the final approach path for traffic and, if clear, start your turn. Roll out on final approach between 300 and 500 feet above ground level, and approximately one-quarter mile from the end of the runway.

> To compensate for overshooting the runway during the turn from base to final, do not use excessive rudder pressure to increase the rate of turn—you risk entering a cross-control stall.
>
> If you are flying an airplane with retractable landing gear, re-check that the landing gear is down and locked.

 Fly a stabilized approach.

- Maintain the recommended approach speed. If an approach speed is not recommended in the AFM/POH, use a final approach speed that is 1.3 times the power-off stall speed in the landing configuration ($1.3V_{S0}$).

- Use outside references to determine the proper descent angle, or glide path.

> If you maintain a constant descent angle, the apparent shape of the runway will remain unchanged. If your approach becomes shallower, the runway will appear to shorten and become wider. Conversely, if your approach is steepened, the runway will appear to be longer and narrower. If you maintain a constant descent angle, the sides of the runway will maintain the same relationship and the threshold will remain in a fixed position in relation to the airplane's nose.

MANEUVER 13 ■ **Normal Approach and Landing**

MANEUVER 13 ■ Normal Approach and Landing

- Simultaneously adjust pitch and power as necessary to control the descent angle and airspeed. If the airplane deviates from the correct pitch attitude or airspeed, or if the wind condition varies, make an appropriate control change to maintain the proper descent angle.

These techniques are recommended to correct for deviations from the correct descent angle and airspeed on final approach.

If the descent angle is too steep (airplane is too high) and the airspeed is:
- Too fast—reduce power and gradually increase the pitch attitude.
- Correct—reduce power and maintain pitch attitude.
- Too slow—reduce power and decrease the pitch attitude.

If the descent angle is too shallow (airplane is too low) and the airspeed is:
- Too fast—increase the pitch attitude and add power, if necessary.
- Correct—add power and maintain the pitch attitude.
- Too slow—add power and decrease the pitch attitude slightly. Increase the power anytime the airplane is low and slow. Do not try to stretch a glide by applying back pressure to increase pitch attitude without adding power.

As you approach the proper descent angle and airspeed after making a correction, readjust the power and pitch to maintain the correct attitude and trim to relieve control pressures.

- Estimate the point at which the airplane will actually touch down by finding the point where the descent angle intersects the ground and adding the approximate distance to be traveled in the flare. The descent angle intersection point, also called the aiming point, is the spot on the ground that has no apparent relative movement. As the airplane descends, all objects beyond the aiming point appear to move away from the airplane, while objects closer appear to move toward it.

Aiming Point (Descent Angle Intersects Ground)

Touchdown

Distance Traveled in Flare

LANDING

During the landing you use a combination of visual and kinesthetic cues. Performing descents, slow flight, and power-off stalls in the practice area helps you develop the proper control responses and smooth control application. However, your kinesthetic sense might not be fully developed at the time you begin landing practice and you must rely primarily on visual cues. The landing consists of three elements — the flare, the touchdown, and the roll-out. The term **flare** refers to the process of changing the attitude of the airplane from a glide or descent to a landing attitude. Its purpose is to reduce speed and decrease the rate of descent. The flare begins at different altitudes for airplanes at varying weights and approach speeds. However, for most training airplanes it begins at approximately 10 to 20 feet above the ground.

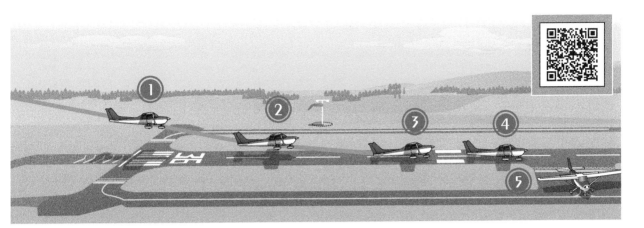

 Begin the flare.

- At approximately 10 to 20 feet above the runway, gradually increase back pressure on the control stick to reduce speed and decrease the rate of descent.

- Focus at an intermediate point between the nose of the airplane and a distance down the runway. During the flare, you must look to one side of the airplane, because its nose can block your view ahead.

② **Establish the proper landing attitude.**

- The airplane should reach a near-zero rate of descent approximately one foot above the runway at about 8 to 10 knots above stall speed with the power at idle.

- Try to hold the airplane just off the runway by increasing back pressure.

> Use a visual comparison of the size of known objects on the ground, or depth perception, to determine the attitude for the flare and the height throughout the flare. The area where you focus your vision during the approach is important. For example, if you focus too close to the airplane, the airspeed blurs objects on the ground and your actions might be too abrupt. If you focus too far down the runway, you might be unable to accurately judge height above the ground and your reactions will be slow. In this situation, you might allow the airplane to fly onto the runway without flaring.

 Touch down.

- Allow the airplane to settle to the runway on the main landing gear. The airplane is in a nose-high attitude, approaching stall speed with the engine idling.

> As the airplane touches down, your heels should be on the floor so there is no tendency to use the brakes inadvertently. Braking on touchdown with the wheels spinning at a fast rate can cause flat spots on the tires.

- Use the rudder to keep the airplane's longitudinal axis parallel to the direction the airplane is moving along the runway.

> You must be alert for the possibility of losing directional control immediately upon and after touchdown due to the ground friction on the wheels. Loss of directional control can lead to a ground loop—an aggravated, uncontrolled, tight turn. The combination of centrifugal force acting on the center of gravity (CG) and ground friction of the main wheels resisting it during the ground loop can cause the airplane to lean enough that the outside wing contacts the ground.

- Hold back pressure on the control stick to maintain a positive angle of attack for aerodynamic braking and to hold the nosewheel off the ground.

- As the airplane decelerates, gradually relax back pressure to allow the nosewheel to gently settle onto the runway.

> Flying the airplane onto the runway with excess speed can cause floating or skipping and can result in a loss of directional control.

MANEUVER 13 ▪ **Normal Approach and Landing**

4 Roll out. Maintain directional control with the rudder to keep the airplane on the centerline of the runway. Slow down without braking excessively.

> As the airplane decelerates, braking can cause the nose to pitch down, which transfers weight from the main wheels to the nose wheel. To increase braking effectiveness, apply back pressure to take weight off of the nosewheel without lifting it off the ground.

5 Clear the runway. Complete the after landing checklist. Taxi to the designated parking or refueling area.

> Ensure the airplane has slowed sufficiently to exit the runway without excessive braking. If the tower directs you to exit at a specific location, inform that you are "unable" if the airplane is not at a safe speed for turning.
>
> To help prevent a runway incursion, ensure you have positional awareness after exiting the runway. At a controlled airport, stay on the tower frequency until instructed to change frequencies.

IV. Takeoffs, Landings, and Go-Arounds

Task	B. Normal Approach and Landing
References	FAA-H-8083-2, FAA-H-8083-3, FAA-H-8083-23; POH/AFM; AIM
Objective	To determine that the applicant exhibits satisfactory knowledge, risk management, and skills associated with a normal approach and landing with emphasis on proper use and coordination of flight controls. **Note:** *If a crosswind condition does not exist, the applicant's knowledge of crosswind elements must be evaluated through oral testing.*
Knowledge	The applicant demonstrates understanding of:
PA.IV.B.K1	A stabilized approach, to include energy management concepts.
PA.IV.B.K2	Effects of atmospheric conditions, including wind, on approach and landing performance.
PA.IV.B.K3	Wind correction techniques on approach and landing.
Risk Management	The applicant demonstrates the ability to identify, assess and mitigate risks, encompassing:
PA.IV.B.R1	Selection of runway based on pilot capability, airplane performance and limitations, available distance, and wind.
PA.IV.B.R2	Effects of:
PA.IV.B.R2a	a. Crosswind
PA.IV.B.R2b	b. Windshear
PA.IV.B.R2c	c. Tailwind
PA.IV.B.R2d	d. Wake turbulence
PA.IV.B.R2e	e. Runway surface/condition
PA.IV.B.R3	Planning for:
PA.IV.B.R3a	a. Go-around and rejected landing.
PA.IV.B.R3b	b. Land and hold short operations (LAHSO)
PA.IV.B.R4	Collision hazards, to include aircraft, vehicles, vessels, persons, wildlife, terrain, obstacles, and wires.
PA.IV.B.R5	Low altitude maneuvering including stall, spin, or CFIT.
PA.IV.B.R6	Distractions, loss of situational awareness, and/or improper task management.
Skills	The applicant demonstrates the ability to:
PA.IV.B.S1	Complete the appropriate checklist.
PA.IV.B.S2	Make radio calls as appropriate.
PA.IV.B.S3	Ensure the airplane is aligned with the correct/assigned runway or landing surface.
PA.IV.B.S4	Scan the runway or landing surface and the adjoining area for traffic and obstructions.
PA.IV.B.S5	Consider the wind conditions, landing surface, obstructions, and select a suitable touchdown point.
PA.IV.B.S6	Establish the recommended approach and landing configuration and airspeed, and adjust pitch attitude and power as required to maintain a stabilized approach.
PA.IV.B.S7	Maintain manufacturer's published approach airspeed or in its absence not more than 1.3 V_{SO}, +10/-5 knots with gust factor applied.
PA.IV.B.S8	Maintain crosswind correction and directional control throughout the approach and landing.
PA.IV.B.S9	Make smooth, timely, and correct control application during round out and touchdown.
PA.IV.B.S10	Touch down at a proper pitch attitude, within 400 feet beyond or on the specified point, with no side drift, and with the airplane's longitudinal axis aligned with and over the runway center/landing path.
PA.IV.B.S11	Execute a timely go-around if the approach cannot be made within the tolerances specified above or for any other condition that may result in an unsafe approach or landing.
PA.IV.B.S12	Utilize runway incursion avoidance procedures.

MANEUVER 13 ■ **Normal Approach and Landing**

ACS

FAULTY LANDINGS

Most likely you will experience some faulty landings. Fortunately, you can take a variety of actions to correct for most errors to save your landing. If you misjudge the sink rate during a landing and think the airplane is descending faster than it should, you might increase the pitch attitude too rapidly and cause the airplane to climb. This climb is known as ballooning.

At times, you also might experience floating when you level off over the runway during landing if the airspeed on final approach is excessive. In this case, the airplane can be well past the desired landing point and the available runway might be insufficient.

An improper attitude or excessive rate of sink can cause the airplane to bounce back into the air due to an abrupt increase in the wing's angle of attack. A improperly recovered bounced landing can lead to porpoising—the airplane strikes the runway nose first initiating a series of motions that imitate the jumps and dives of a porpoise. Correcting for a porpoise is the same as for a bounce and depends on its severity. If the porpoise is severe, the airplane's pitch oscillations can become progressively worse until the airplane strikes the runway nose first with sufficient force to collapse the nose gear. Attempts to correct a severe porpoise with flight control and power inputs can make the situation worse so you must immediately perform a go-around. The causes and corrections for faulty landings are shown in the following table.

FAULTY LANDINGS	CAUSES	CORRECTIONS
Ballooning	Too much back pressure Excess airspeed Excess power	Small balloon—hold the pitch attitude and let the airplane settle to the runway. Large balloon—relax some back pressure until the airplane descends to flare height. Then add back pressure and complete a normal landing. Excessive balloon—add full power to go around.
Floating	Excess airspeed Excess power	Reduce the power to idle and hold the airplane off the runway to bleed off excess airspeed. If you cannot land on the first third of the runway, add full power to go around.
Bouncing	Adding too much back pressure when trying to fix an incorrect landing attitude during touchdown Touching down with excess airspeed Stalling a few feet above the runway and letting the airplane touch down hard	Small bounce or porpoise—adjust the pitch attitude and add power to maintain airspeed and cushion the next touchdown. Extreme bounce or porpoise—add full power to go around.

MANEUVER 13 ■ Normal Approach and Landing

14 — Forward Slip to a Landing

You can use a forward slip to steepen the airplane's descent angle to dissipate altitude without increasing airspeed. This is accomplished by exposing as much of the airplane's surface to the oncoming air as possible, so the airplane's frontal area produces considerable drag. A forward slip can be valuable when you are landing in fields with obstructions. In an airplane with side-by-side seating, you will usually slip to the left since this provides you with an excellent view of the landing area during the entire slip.

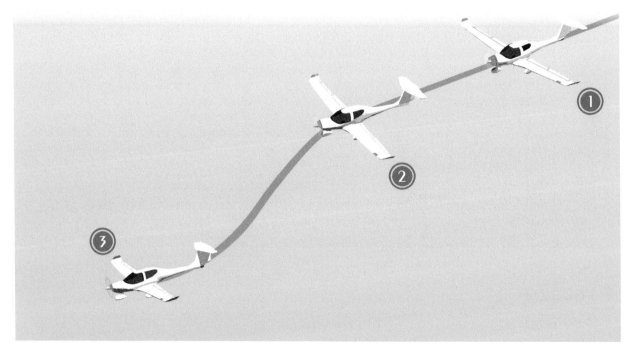

MANEUVER 14 ■ Forward Slip to a Landing

① **Establish the slip attitude.** Reduce power to idle and establish a glide toward the runway or landing area. Use the control stick to lower one wing. Apply opposite rudder to keep the airplane from turning in the direction of the lowered wing. To prevent the airspeed from increasing, raise the nose slightly above the normal gliding position.

> The airplane's nose will angle away from the runway. However, the airplane's ground track remains in alignment with the extended centerline of the runway.
>
> Be aware that airspeed indicators in some airplanes can have considerable error when the airplane is in a slip due to the location of the pitot tube and static port. You must recognize a properly performed slip by the attitude, the sound of the airflow, and the feel of the flight controls.

② **Establish the desired rate of descent and airspeed.** Increase or decrease the bank angle and rudder deflection to increase or decrease the rate of descent, respectively. Adjust the pitch to maintain the appropriate airspeed—best glide speed or approach speed.

> If you are applying full rudder to maintain heading even though the ailerons are capable of further steepening the bank angle, you have reached the practical slip limit because any additional bank would cause the airplane to turn even though you are applying full opposite rudder. If you need to descend more rapidly, lowering the nose not only increases the sink rate but also increases airspeed which in turn increases rudder effectiveness permitting a steeper slip. Conversely, when the nose is raised, rudder effectiveness decreases and you must reduce the bank angle.

③ **Recover from the slip after losing sufficient altitude.** Raise the low wing while releasing the opposite rudder pressure. Adjust the pitch to maintain the appropriate airspeed.

> If you release rudder pressure too abruptly, the nose swings too quickly into line and the airplane tends to gain excess speed.

Another type of slip is the sideslip, which is used to compensate for drift during crosswind landings. During a sideslip, the airplane's longitudinal axis remains parallel to the original flight path and is aligned with the runway. You will learn more about performing sideslips when you examine Maneuver 16 — Crosswind Approach and Landing.

IV. Takeoffs, Landings, and Go-Arounds

Task	M. Forward Slip to a Landing (ASEL, ASES)
References	FAA-H-8083-2, FAA-H-8083-3; POH/AFM; AIM
Objective	To determine that the applicant exhibits satisfactory knowledge, risk management, and skills associated with a forward slip to a landing.
Knowledge	The applicant demonstrates understanding of:
PA.IV.M.K1	Concepts of energy management during a forward slip approach.
PA.IV.M.K2	Effects of atmospheric conditions, including wind, on approach and landing performance.
PA.IV.M.K3	Wind correction techniques during forward slip.
PA.IV.M.K4	When and why a forward slip approach is used during an approach.
Risk Management	The applicant demonstrates the ability to identify, assess and mitigate risks, encompassing:
PA.IV.M.R1	Selection of runway or approach path and touchdown area based on pilot capability, airplane performance and limitations, available distance, and wind.
PA.IV.M.R2	Effects of:
PA.IV.M.R2a	a. Crosswind
PA.IV.M.R2b	b. Windshear
PA.IV.M.R2c	c. Tailwind
PA.IV.M.R2d	d. Wake turbulence
PA.IV.M.R2e	e. Runway surface/condition
PA.IV.M.R3	Planning for go-around and rejected landing.
PA.IV.M.R3a	a. Rejected takeoff
PA.IV.M.R3b	b. Engine failure in takeoff/climb phase of flight
PA.IV.M.R4	Collision hazards, to include aircraft, vehicles, vessels, persons, wildlife, terrain, obstacles, and wires.
PA.IV.M.R5	Low altitude maneuvering including stall, spin, or CFIT.
PA.IV.M.R6	Distractions, loss of situational awareness, and/or improper task management.
PA.IV.M.R7	Forward slip operations, including fuel flowage, tail stalls with flaps, and lack of airspeed control.
PA.IV.M.R8	Surface contact with the airplane's longitudinal axis misaligned.
PA.IV.M.R9	Unstable approach.
Skills	The applicant demonstrates the ability to:
PA.IV.M.S1	Complete the appropriate checklist.
PA.IV.M.S2	Make radio calls as appropriate.
PA.IV.M.S3	Plan and follow a flightpath to the selected landing area considering altitude, wind, terrain, and obstructions.
PA.IV.M.S4	Select the most suitable touchdown point based on wind, landing surface, obstructions, and airplane limitations.
PA.IV.M.S5	Position airplane on downwind leg, parallel to landing runway.
PA.IV.M.S6	Configure the airplane correctly.
PA.IV.M.S7	As necessary, correlate crosswind with direction of forward slip and transition to side slip before touchdown.
PA.IV.M.S8	Touch down at a proper pitch attitude, within 400 feet beyond or on the specified point, with no side drift, and with the airplane's longitudinal axis aligned with and over the runway center/landing path.
PA.IV.M.S9	Maintain a ground track aligned with the runway center/landing path.

MANEUVER 14 ■ Forward Slip to a Landing

MANEUVER 15 ■ Go-Around

15 — Go-Around

Generally, if you have not established a stabilized approach on final or if the airplane has not touched down in the first third of the runway, you should perform a go-around, and set up for another landing. A go-around also might be necessary when an unsafe condition exists, such as an animal, aircraft or vehicle on the runway, wind shear or wake turbulence on final approach, or a faulty landing. In addition, at a controlled airport, the tower might instruct you to go around for traffic spacing purposes. Your decision to go around must be positive and made before a critical situation develops. After you have decided to go around, implement your decision without hesitation. Do not believe that going around is an admission of failure.

 Stop the descent. Apply takeoff power *immediately*, turn the carburetor heat to COLD (if applicable), and adjust the airplane's pitch attitude to stop the descent. After stopping the descent, partially retract the flaps (if applicable) as recommended by the manufacturer.

> When you apply full power, you normally must hold a considerable amount of forward pressure on the control stick because the airplane was trimmed for approach. In addition, you must apply right rudder pressure to counteract torque and P-factor. To help keep the airplane in a safe climbing attitude, trim the airplane to relieve the heavy control pressures.
>
> Use caution when retracting the flaps. Normally, you retract the flaps in small increments to allow the airplane to accelerate as the flaps are raised. Retracting the flaps prematurely causes a loss of lift that could result in the airplane settling back to the runway.

 Initiate a climb. Adjust the pitch attitude to establish a positive rate of climb at V_Y or V_X. If another aircraft is on the runway, make a shallow turn to the side of the runway, then turn parallel to the runway. In this position, you can see the runway and other aircraft clearly.

> When initiating a go-around close to the ground, be aware of the apparent increase in performance due to ground effect. Increasing the pitch too quickly could prevent the airplane from climbing or even maintaining altitude.
>
> Special cases, such as the use of parallel runways, might prevent you from making a turn to the side of the runway.

Stabilize the climb. Retract the landing gear (if applicable), and accelerate to V_Y before retracting the remaining flaps. Maintain directional control and apply proper wind drift as you continue the flight parallel to the departure leg. Trim to relieve control pressures.

Because full flaps produce more drag than extended landing gear, it is generally recommended that you partially retract the flaps before retracting the landing gear. This action also prevents damage if the airplane inadvertently touches down on the runway as you initiate the go-around.

 Make the appropriate radio call after you have reached a safe altitude, Announce your position and intentions on the CTAF or tower frequency.

 Transition to the traffic pattern. When you reach the crosswind leg, allow for proper spacing, check for traffic, and then reenter the traffic pattern as appropriate.

MANEUVER 15 ▪ **Go-Around**

IV. Takeoffs, Landings, and Go-Arounds

Task	N. Go-Around/Rejected Landing
References	FAA-H-8083-3, FAA-H-8083-23; POH/AFM; AIM
Objective	To determine that the applicant exhibits satisfactory knowledge, risk management, and skills associated with a go-around/rejected landing with emphasis on factors that contribute to landing conditions that may require a go-around.
Knowledge	The applicant demonstrates understanding of:
PA.IV.N.K1	A stabilized approach, to include energy management concepts.
PA.IV.N.K2	Effects of atmospheric conditions, including wind and density altitude on a go-around or rejected landing.
PA.IV.N.K3	Wind correction techniques on takeoff/departure and approach/landing.
Risk Management	The applicant demonstrates the ability to identify, assess and mitigate risks, encompassing:
PA.IV.N.R1	Delayed recognition of the need for a go-around/rejected landing.
PA.IV.N.R2	Delayed performance of a go-around at low altitude.
PA.IV.N.R3	Improper application of power.
PA.IV.N.R4	Improper airplane configuration.
PA.IV.N.R5	Collision hazards, to include aircraft, vehicles, vessels, persons, wildlife, terrain, obstacles, and wires.
PA.IV.N.R6	Low altitude maneuvering including stall, spin, or CFIT.
PA.IV.N.R7	Distractions, loss of situational awareness, and/or improper task management.
Skills	The applicant demonstrates the ability to:
PA.IV.N.S1	Complete the appropriate checklist.
PA.IV.N.S2	Make radio calls as appropriate.
PA.IV.N.S3	Make a timely decision to discontinue the approach to landing.
PA.IV.N.S4	Apply takeoff power immediately and transition to climb pitch attitude for V_X or V_Y as appropriate +10/-5 knots.
PA.IV.N.S5	Configure the airplane after a positive rate of climb has been verified or in accordance with airplane manufacturer's instructions.
PA.IV.N.S6	Maneuver to the side of the runway/landing area when necessary to clear and avoid conflicting traffic.
PA.IV.N.S7	Maintain V_Y +10/-5 knots to a safe maneuvering altitude.
PA.IV.N.S8	Maintain directional control and proper wind-drift correction throughout the climb.

16 — Crosswind Approach and Landing

Two basic techniques to perform a crosswind approach and landing are the crab method and the wing-low, or sideslip, method. The crab method requires you to establish a heading (crab) into the wind on final approach with the wings level so that the airplane's ground track remains aligned with the extended centerline of the runway. The crab angle is maintained until just prior to touchdown, when you must quickly align the airplane's longitudinal axis with the runway to avoid imposing any side loads on the main landing gear.

Because the crab method requires a high degree of judgment and timing, the wing-low method is normally preferred for performing crosswind landings. The wing-low method of crosswind approach and landing is described here. The wing-low method enables you to simultaneously keep the airplane's ground track and the longitudinal axis aligned with the runway centerline throughout the final approach, flare, touchdown, and roll-out. This technique prevents the airplane from touching down sideways, which can impose damaging side loads on the landing gear.

The degree to which you should extend flaps in a crosswind varies with the airplane's handling characteristics, the wind velocity and the manufacturer's guidelines. In addition, refer to the AFM/POH for the maximum demonstrated crosswind velocity for takeoff and landing. Until you have gained sufficient practice and experience with crosswind landings, you should apply a personal limitation that is less than this speed. Base your crosswind limit on your skill level and any restrictions specified by your instructor or by the aircraft operator. Because the same general procedures that you use to perform a normal approach and landing apply to a crosswind approach and landing, only the additional techniques required for wind correction are explained in this discussion.

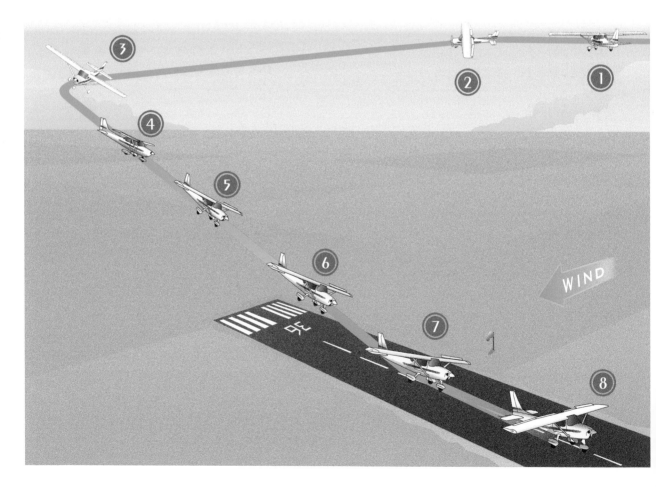

(1) Maintain the proper ground track on downwind. If the crosswind exists at traffic pattern altitude and near the surface, you must apply the proper wind correction (crab) in the traffic pattern so your ground track remains rectangular. Because the wind direction is perpendicular to the runway, you must crab into the wind on the downwind leg to remain parallel to the runway at the correct distance.

(2) Adjust for wind drift as you turn base. If the airplane is crabbed toward the runway on downwind, turn less than 90° onto base; if crabbed away from the runway, turn more than 90°.

(3) Adjust for wind drift turning final. If you have a tailwind on base, turn early and use up to 30° of bank to avoid overshooting the runway. With a headwind on base, turn later than usual and use a shallow bank to avoid undershooting the runway.

(4) Crab into the wind as you roll out on final. Complete the turn to final on an extension of the runway centerline with the airplane in a crab to correct for wind drift.

(5) Transition to the sideslip (wing-low) method of crosswind correction. Align the airplane's heading with the runway centerline, and then correct sideways drift by lowering the upwind wing. Continue applying opposite rudder to prevent the airplane from turning and to keep the longitudinal axis aligned with the runway. For example, if the crosswind is blowing from your left, move the control wheel to the left and apply right rudder.

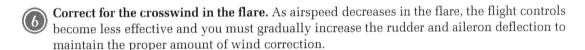

If the crosswind diminishes, you must reduce the wind correction or the airplane will no longer be aligned with the runway centerline. If the crosswind is very strong, you might not have sufficient rudder travel available to compensate for the strong turning tendency caused by the lowered wing. In this situation, you must go around and land on a runway with more favorable wind conditions.

(6) Correct for the crosswind in the flare. As airspeed decreases in the flare, the flight controls become less effective and you must gradually increase the rudder and aileron deflection to maintain the proper amount of wind correction.

(7) Touch down maintaining the crosswind correction. Initially, the airplane will touch down on the upwind wheel and then as forward momentum decreases, the weight of the airplane causes the downwind main wheel to gradually settle onto the runway. Gradually relax back pressure to allow the nosewheel to gently settle on the runway.

If the airplane has nosewheel steering interconnected with the rudder, the nosewheel will not be aligned with the runway as the airplane touches down because you are holding opposite rudder pressure to correct for the crosswind. To prevent swerving on the runway, relax the corrective rudder pressure just as the nosewheel touches down.

(8) Roll out maintaining the crosswind correction.

- Maintain directional control with the rudder while keeping the upwind wing from rising by maintaining aileron deflection into the wind.

- As the airplane decelerates and the controls become less effective, increase your wind correction with the ailerons. Move the control wheel fully into the wind as the airplane slows to a taxi speed. Clear the runway and complete the after landing checklist.

The Private Pilot Airman Certification Standards (ACS) for the Normal Approach and Landing task also apply to crosswind approach and landing. See page 3-18.

MANEUVER 16 ▪ Crosswind Approach and Landing

MANEUVER 16 ■ Crosswind Approach and Landing

EXERCISES — AIRPORT OPERATIONS

10 — NORMAL TAKEOFF AND CLIMB

1. How can you counteract the left-turning tendency caused by engine torque on takeoff?

_____

2. Why should you keep your hand on the throttle throughout the takeoff?

_____

3. What can occur if you attempt to lift off with an excessively nose-high attitude?

_____

4. After a normal takeoff at an uncontrolled airport, what are the recommended procedures for leaving the local area?

_____

5. What action should you take if the engine is not developing sufficient power for takeoff?

_____

11 — CROSSWIND TAKEOFF AND CLIMB

1. How can you determine the maximum demonstrated crosswind velocity for your airplane?

_____

2. True/False. To counteract the effects of a crosswind from the left during takeoff, you should move the control wheel to the right, placing the left aileron in the down position.

3. As the airplane accelerates during the takeoff roll, will you normally need to increase or decrease aileron deflection used to compensate for a crosswind?_____

4. How can you determine if you are using the proper amount of crosswind correction?

_____

5. After takeoff, what action can you take to track straight out on an imaginary extension of the runway centerline?

_____

12 — TRAFFIC PATTERNS

1. What are the five named legs of the traffic pattern?

    _____

2. True/False. Both left-hand and right-hand traffic patterns are normally used when simultaneous operations are conducted on parallel runways.

3. To aid in collision avoidance, you should turn on your airplane's landing light within how many miles of the airport? _____

4. In the absence of a UNICOM operator or operating control tower, how can you determine the landing runway and the associated pattern direction?

    _____

5. Your airplane is Piper 9163K and you are practicing touch-and-go landings to Runway 26 at Boulder Airport (uncontrolled). Provide an example of the proper radio call after completing the turn to final.

    _____

13 — NORMAL APPROACH AND LANDING

1. True/False. Landing with full flaps extended results in a faster touchdown speed and ground roll.

2. At what position on the downwind leg should you normally begin your descent for landing?

    _____

3. What corrective actions can you take if the airplane is high when you reach the key position?

    _____

4. While on final approach, if the airplane's descent angle is too shallow and the airspeed is too slow, what action should you take?

    _____

5. The landing phase of flight can be divided into what three elements?

    _____

6. While maintaining directional control with the rudder pedals, why should your heels be on the floor as the airplane touches down?

    _____

7. During landing, floating can be caused by what?

    _____

14 — FORWARD SLIP TO A LANDING

1. What is the primary purpose of the forward slip?

2. True/False. While performing a forward slip, the airplane's longitudinal axis is aligned with the runway.

3. How do you set the power and position the controls to establish a forward slip?

15 — GO-AROUND

1. Name at least 3 reasons to perform a go-around.

2. What is the first step you should take when initiating a go-around?

3. Which is true regarding performing a go-around?
   A. When you apply full power, you normally have to apply back pressure to climb.
   B. You must apply right rudder pressure to counteract torque and P-factor when adding power.
   C. When initiating a go-around close to the ground, you should increase the pitch and retract the flaps as quickly as possible to climb out of ground effect.

16 — CROSSWIND APPROACH AND LANDING

1. What are the two basic methods used for crosswind approach and landings?

2. If you experience a tailwind on base leg, what action(s) can you take to avoid overshooting the runway when turning onto final approach?

3. If you encounter a crosswind from the right on final approach and landing, how should you position the controls to compensate for wind drift?
   A. Move the control wheel/stick to the left and apply left rudder pressure.
   B. Move the control wheel/stick to the left and apply right rudder pressure.
   C. Move the control wheel/stick to the right and apply left rudder pressure.

4. While making a crosswind correction on final approach, what action should you take if you do not have sufficient rudder travel available?

5. As the airplane decelerates during the roll-out, will you need to increase or decrease aileron deflection to counteract a steady crosswind?

EXERCISES ■ **Airport Operations**

CHAPTER 4

Emergency Operations

17 — Systems and Equipment Malfunctions

Your airplane's AFM/POH contains checklists for abnormal and emergency procedures to manage systems and equipment malfunctions. You typically use one of two methods for following these checklists depending on the urgency of the situation. With a do-list, you read the checklist item and the associated action and then perform the action. Use a do-list to address a minor malfunction that does not required immediate action. For more serious malfunctions, emergency checklists typically include tasks that you must perform from memory before referring to the checklist.

Always refer to the AFM/POH checklist to manage a systems and equipment malfunction. However, in the absence of a specific procedure in the AFM/POH, follow FAA recommendations. Do not hesitate to contact ATC to advise the controller of your situation, seek assistance, or declare an emergency. The following discussion provides general considerations for managing systems and equipment malfunctions.

PARTIAL POWER LOSS

Maneuver 19 — Emergency Approach and Landing addresses a complete power loss. However, you also can experience a partial power loss. Your AFM/POH might contain procedures for troubleshooting and restoring power after experiencing a partial power loss or engine roughness. Depending on the airplane, causes for a partial power loss can include: carburetor ice, partial failure of the engine driven fuel pump, fouled spark plugs, vapor in the fuel lines, and partial blockage of the intake air.

If you are unable to restore power, you must make a decision of how to proceed based on the cause of the power loss, the power available, airplane performance, and the flight environment. If the airplane can maintain altitude or climb, you might be able to continue the flight to a nearby airport in a reduced power condition. In this situation, maintain an airspeed that provides the best airplane performance available—approximately the best glide speed in many airplanes.

If your airplane's performance with partial power is not sufficient to maintain altitude or the cause of the power loss is severe enough that an engine failure is imminent, consider performing an off-airport precautionary landing. Partial power can provide you more time for terrain selection and approach planning than you would have with a complete engine failure. With any engine problem, continually monitor the engine instruments, update your choice of landing options, and be prepared to perform an emergency approach and landing.

MANAGING MALFUNCTIONS

ELECTRICAL SYSTEM MALFUNCTION

If the ammeter or loadmeter (depending on the airplane) or an annunciation indicates a possible alternator failure, follow the steps outlined in your AFM/POH to reset the alternator. If the alternator remains off line, the electrical source in the typical training airplane is the battery, which has a limited charge. Consider these actions to manage an alternator failure:

- Determine the essential electrical equipment for the flight and severity of the situation based on factors such as VFR or IFR conditions, day or night, and distance from an airport.

- Shed electrical load to preserve battery power for essential equipment.

- Notify ATC of the situation and use ATC services, such as radar vectors, as appropriate.

- Be prepared to control the airplane and land without primary instrumentation (in the case of digital instrument displays), radio communication, lights, or flaps, and to perform a manual landing gear extension, if applicable.

GYROSCOPIC INSTRUMENT MALFUNCTION

In an airplane with analog instruments, a vacuum/pressure system malfunction affects the attitude indicator and heading indicator. In IFR conditions, a failure of these instruments is an emergency and you are trained to control the airplane by referring to a partial panel. However, in VFR conditions, you maintain aircraft attitude using outside references and use the magnetic compass for heading information. In an airplane with a primary flight display (PFD), an attitude and heading reference system (AHRS) failure causes red Xs to cover the attitude indicator and the horizontal situation indicator (HSI). In this situation, use outside visual references, the backup analog attitude indicator, and the magnetic compass for reference. The Jeppesen *Private Pilot* textbook provides more detailed information on these systems.

PITOT/STATIC SYSTEM MALFUNCTION

If you lose pitot-static data in an airplane with a PFD, typically red Xs cover the affected instruments. However, there are a variety of indications of pitot-static system blockage on analog instruments. If you suspect a possible blockage of the pitot-static system based on instrument indications consider taking these actions:

- If the static source is blocked, open the alternate static source.

- If the pitot tube is blocked, apply pitot heat.

- Use outside visual references to control the airplane.

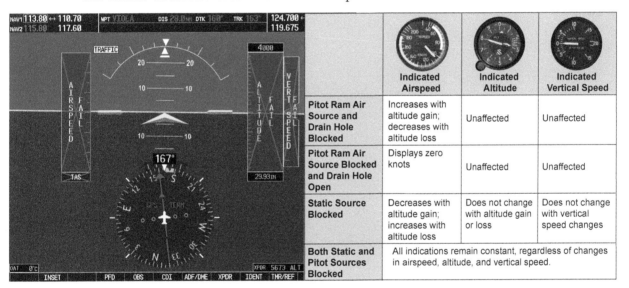

	Indicated Airspeed	Indicated Altitude	Indicated Vertical Speed
Pitot Ram Air Source and Drain Hole Blocked	Increases with altitude gain; decreases with altitude loss	Unaffected	Unaffected
Pitot Ram Air Source Blocked and Drain Hole Open	Displays zero knots	Unaffected	Unaffected
Static Source Blocked	Decreases with altitude gain; increases with altitude loss	Does not change with altitude gain or loss	Does not change with vertical speed changes
Both Static and Pitot Sources Blocked	All indications remain constant, regardless of changes in airspeed, altitude, and vertical speed.		

ELECTRONIC FLIGHT DECK DISPLAY MALFUNCTION

The integrated flight display is configured so that the functions of the PFD can be transferred to the multifunction display (MFD), and vice versa. If the PFD screen turns black, the PFD instruments should automatically display on the MFD in reversionary mode. In the event that the PFD does not appear on the MFD, most systems enable you to manually switch to reversionary mode.

FLAP MALFUNCTION

You enter the traffic pattern and the flaps do not extend. There are several factors to consider as you prepare to perform a no-flap approach and landing:

- The glide path is not as steep as with flaps extended, so the higher nose attitude on final can cause errors in your judgment of height and distance.

- Landing distance is substantially increased.

- Floating during the flare is likely.

Although rare, an unexpected rolling motion during flap extension can be caused by an asymmetrical or split flap condition. If one flap extends while the other remains in place, a differential in lift across the wing is the cause of the rolling motion. A split flap condition can be hazardous, particularly in the traffic pattern or during a turn at low altitude. Counter the roll with opposite aileron and fly the approach to landing at a higher than normal airspeed. Fly the airplane so that the touchdown occurs at an airspeed consistent with a safe margin above flaps-up stall speed.

LANDING GEAR MALFUNCTION

Follow the steps in the AFM/POH for your specific airplane to manually extend the landing gear. If all efforts to extend the landing gear fail and a gear-up landing is inevitable, select an airport with crash and rescue facilities—do not hesitate to request that emergency equipment be standing by. If only one landing gear leg fails to extend, you might have the option of landing on the available gear legs or landing with all the gear legs retracted. Consider these actions:

- All gear legs retracted—landing with all three gear retracted might be the safest course of action depending on the airplane and runway environment. Consider burning off excess fuel to reduce the landing speed and fire potential.

- Landing on one main gear—land in a nose-high attitude with the wings level. Apply aileron control to keep the unsupported wing airborne as long as possible. After the wing contacts the surface, be prepared to use full opposite rudder and aggressive braking to maintain directional control.

- Retracted nosewheel with the main gear extended and locked—hold the nose off the ground until almost full up-elevator has been applied. Then, gradually release back pressure so that the nose settles slowly to the surface.

- Nose gear only extended—make initial contact on the aft fuselage structure with a nose-high attitude to help prevent porpoising and/or wheelbarrowing. Then, allow the nosewheel to gradually touch down.

LOSS OF ELEVATOR CONTROL

If the linkage between the cabin and the elevator fails in flight—leaving the elevator free to weathervane in the wind—you typically can use trim to raise or lower the elevator within limits. The trim tab is not as effective as normal linkage control at low airspeeds but you can usually land safely. If an elevator becomes jammed—resulting in a total loss of elevator control movement—you must use various combinations of power and flap extensions for a limited amount of pitch control. Refer to the AFM/POH for your airplane's specific procedures to land without elevator control.

INOPERATIVE TRIM

An aural and/or visual warning normally signals you to an electric trim malfunction associated with either manual or autopilot trim. If you experience a trim malfunction, immediately grasp the control wheel to control the airplane. If you cannot correct the problem and are experiencing runaway trim, pull the applicable circuit breakers as recommended by the AFM/POH and land as soon as practical.

SMOKE AND FIRE

If you experience a fire while in flight, follow the checklist procedures specified in the AFM/POH for your airplane and declare an emergency by radio. The checklist might address only one type of in-flight fire or it might include procedures for different types of fires ranging from cabin and electrical fires to engine fires. Managing smoke or fire in the cabin typically involves these actions:

- Turn off the master switch to remove the possible source of the fire.

- If flames exist, use the fire extinguisher to put out the fire.

- After extinguishing the fire, open the air vents to clear the cabin of smoke and fumes.

- Land as soon as possible.

DOOR OPENING IN FLIGHT

A cabin or baggage compartment door opening in flight can be a disconcerting event. Although a door generally does not open very far, the sudden noise can be startling. Regardless of the noise and confusion, you must maintain control of the airplane, particularly during departure. Accidents have occurred on takeoff because pilots have stopped flying the airplane to concentrate on closing cabin or baggage doors. Consider these factors when managing an inadvertent door opening during flight:

- Stay calm and maintain control of the airplane; an open door is normally not hazardous unless you allow it to distract you.

- Do not release your shoulder harness in an attempt to reach the door,

- Close the door safely on the ground after landing as soon as practical by performing a normal traffic pattern and landing.

IX. Emergency Operations

Task	C. Systems and Equipment Malfunctions
References	FAA-H-8083-2, FAA-H-8083-3; POH/AFM
Objective	To determine that the applicant exhibits satisfactory knowledge, risk management, and skills associated with system and equipment malfunctions appropriate to the airplane provided for the practical test and analyzing the situation and take appropriate action for simulated emergencies.
Knowledge	The applicant demonstrates understanding of:
PA.IX.C.K1	Partial or complete power loss related to the specific powerplant, including:
PA.IX.C.K1a	a. Engine roughness or overheat
PA.IX.C.K1b	b. Carburetor or induction icing
PA.IX.C.K1c	c. Loss of oil pressure
PA.IX.C.K1d	d. Fuel starvation
PA.IX.C.K2	System and equipment malfunctions specific to the airplane, including:
PA.IX.C.K2a	a. Electrical malfunction
PA.IX.C.K2b	b. Vacuum/pressure and associated flight instrument malfunctions
PA.IX.C.K2c	c. Pitot/static system malfunction
PA.IX.C.K2d	d. Electronic flight deck display malfunction
PA.IX.C.K2e	e. Landing gear or flap malfunction
PA.IX.C.K2f	f. Inoperative trim
PA.IX.C.K3	Smoke/fire/engine compartment fire.
PA.IX.C.K4	Any other system specific to the airplane (e.g., supplemental oxygen, deicing).
PA.IX.C.K5	Inadvertent door or window opening.
Risk Management	The applicant demonstrates the ability to identify, assess and mitigate risks, encompassing:
PA.IX.C.R1	Failure to use the proper checklist for a system or equipment malfunction.
PA.IX.C.R2	Distractions, loss of situational awareness, and/or improper task management.
Skills	The applicant demonstrates the ability to:
PA.IX.C.S1	Describe appropriate action for simulated emergencies specified by the evaluator, from at least three of the elements or sub-elements listed in K1 through K5 above.
PA.IX.C.S2	Complete the appropriate checklist.

ACS

MANEUVER 17 ■ Systems and Equipment Malfunctions

18 — Emergency Descent

An emergency descent is a maneuver for descending to a lower altitude as rapidly as possible within the structural limitations of the airplane. You might need to perform an emergency descent due to an uncontrollable fire, smoke in the cockpit, a sudden loss of cabin pressurization, or any other situation that demands an immediate rapid descent. You should complete an emergency descent with sufficient altitude to set up for a precautionary or emergency landing. Perform an emergency descent using the airplane configuration, power setting, and airspeed recommended by the AFM/POH. Do not allow the airplane to exceed the never-exceed speed (V_{NE}), maximum landing gear extended speed (V_{LE}), maximum flap extended speed (V_{FE}), or maneuvering speed (V_A), as applicable.

 Configure the airplane to descend. Reduce the power to idle. Place the propeller control (if equipped) to the low-pitch/high-RPM position and extend the landing gear and flaps, as recommended by the AFM/POH.

> Placing the propeller control (if equipped) in the low-pitch/high-RPM position allows the propeller to act as an aerodynamic brake to help prevent an excessive airspeed buildup during the descent.

 Establish a descending turn. Bank approximately 30° to 45° to maintain a positive load factor on the airplane and increase the rate of descent. Turning also helps you scan for traffic below and look for a possible emergency landing site.

 Maintain the bank angle and maximum allowable airspeed. Ensure that you have completed the Emergency Descent checklist and any other checklists specific to the emergency and maintain:

- V_{NE} for a clean aircraft, with no structural damage, in smooth air.

- V_A for a clean aircraft, with no structural damage, in turbulent air.

- V_{FE} or V_{LE} whichever is more restrictive and applicable to the aircraft configuration recommended by the AFM/POH.

> Consider several additional factors when selecting the descent airspeed. In the case of an engine fire, a high airspeed descent could blow out the fire. However, descending at a low airspeed would place less stress on a weakening airplane structure.

 Return to straight-and-level flight. Roll out of the bank. Gradually raise the nose approximately 100 feet prior to the desired leveloff altitude. Retract the flaps and landing gear (as appropriate).

> Generally, a 10% lead is sufficient for leveloff. For example, 10% of a 1,000 ft/min descent would yield a 100-foot lead for leveloff.

 Return to cruise flight or prepare for landing.

- To return to cruise flight, adjust the power and mixture to the cruise setting and trim to relieve control pressures.

- To prepare for landing, head toward an appropriate site, configure the airplane for landing and maintain approach airspeed.

Level off at a high enough altitude to ensure a safe recovery back to straight-and-level flight or to initiate a precautionary or emergency landing.

During training, you should terminate the procedure when the descent is stabilized and the Emergency Descent checklist is complete. In airplanes with piston engines, avoid prolonged practice of emergency descents to prevent excessive cooling of the engine cylinders.

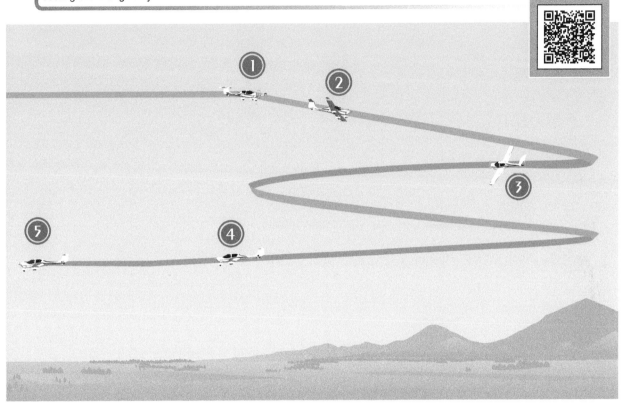

MANEUVER 18 ■ **Emergency Descent**

ACS

IX. Emergency Operations

Task	A. Emergency Descent
References	FAA-H-8083-2, FAA-H-8083-3; POH/AFM
Objective	To determine that the applicant exhibits satisfactory knowledge, risk management, and skills associated with an emergency descent. **Note:** See Appendix 6: Safety of Flight.
Knowledge	The applicant demonstrates understanding of:
PA.IX.A.K1	Situations that require an emergency descent (e.g., depressurization, smoke, and/or engine fire).
PA.IX.A.K2	Immediate action items and emergency procedures.
PA.IX.A.K3	Airspeed, to include airspeed limitations.
Risk Management	The applicant demonstrates the ability to identify, assess and mitigate risks, encompassing:
PA.IX.A.R1	Failure to consider altitude, wind, terrain, obstructions, and available glide distance.
PA.IX.A.R2	Collision hazards, to include aircraft, terrain, obstacles, and wires.
PA.IX.A.R3	Improper airplane configuration.
PA.IX.A.R4	Distractions, loss of situational awareness, and/or improper task management.
Skills	The applicant demonstrates the ability to:
PA.IX.A.S1	Clear the area.
PA.IX.A.S2	Establish and maintain the appropriate airspeed and configuration appropriate to the scenario specified by the evaluator and as covered in POH/AFM for the emergency descent.
PA.IX.A.S3	Demonstrate orientation, division of attention and proper planning.
PA.IX.A.S4	Use bank angle between 30° and 45° to maintain positive load factors during the descent.
PA.IX.A.S5	Maintain appropriate airspeed +0/-10 knots, and level off at a specified altitude ±100 feet.
PA.IX.A.S6	Complete the appropriate checklist.

19 —Emergency Approach and Landing

Modern airplane engines are extremely reliable and actual mechanical malfunctions are rare. However, due to inadvertent fuel exhaustion or an engine component malfunction you could find yourself making an emergency approach and landing. To help you respond quickly to an emergency, some checklists have immediate action items underlined or in bold type that you should perform immediately from memory. In addition, always maintain situational awareness and be constantly on the alert for suitable emergency landing fields. The following guidelines, as well as frequent practice with your flight instructor, will help you develop the ability to plan for an engine failure and methodically perform emergency landing procedures.

LANDING AFTER AN ENGINE FAILURE

Typically, you initially perform simulated engine failures followed by an emergency approach and landing at different altitudes in the practice area. Because most practice emergency landing approaches terminate in a go-around, do not consider the procedure just another training exercise and then be unprepared if an emergency landing situation actually occurs. Assume that each simulated emergency could actually result in a landing.

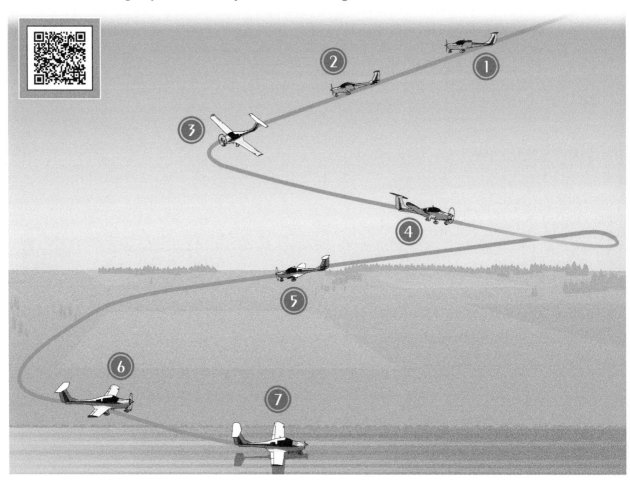

① **Establish a glide.** If you experience an engine failure, maintain control of the airplane and pitch for best glide speed in the AFM/POH. After you reach best glide speed, trim to relieve control pressures and to aid in maintaining the proper attitude and airspeed.

> Attaining best glide speed is an immediate action item. Normally, you must apply back pressure to slow the airplane to the appropriate gliding attitude and speed. However, if your airspeed is below the best glide speed at the time of the engine failure, lower the nose immediately to obtain best glide speed. Properly trimming the airplane is key to maintaining best glide speed during this high workload, high stress situation.

Select a landing site within gliding distance.

- When selecting a field, you must consider the wind direction and speed, length of the field, obstructions, and surface condition. A long field positioned into the wind, with a firm, smooth surface that is free of obstructions is the most desirable.

- Avoid fields which have large boulders, ditches, or other landing hazards. If you choose a plowed field, you should land parallel to the furrows. When considering a road, watch for power lines, signs, and automobile traffic.

- Evaluate your options if a field with ideal landing features is not available. For example, a crosswind landing on a long field might be better than attempting to land into the wind on a very short field. On another occasion, you might prefer to land downwind with light winds and no obstructions rather than land into the wind with numerous obstacles.

> Do not limit your search for a landing field to the terrain ahead of the airplane because you might have just flown by a field better suited for landing. In a low-wing airplane, the wing blocks the area to the right and left of the airplane so make shallow turns to scan the area.

Turn toward the emergency landing site.

- Prepare to dissipate any excess altitude near the field so you are in a good position to look for wires, fences, holes, tree stumps, or other hazards. By waiting to circle over the field, you can make adjustments for altitude while maintaining a position from which you can reach the field.

- Advise your passengers to fasten their seat belts and shoulder harnesses.

Remember, turning upwind reduces your groundspeed and glide distance. Conversely, turning downwind increases your groundspeed and glide distance. Because estimating glide distance is difficult, do not circle away from the landing site and then try to make a long straight-in glide to the field.

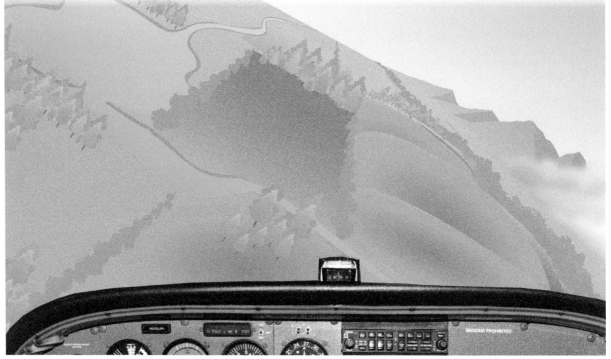

(4) Try to restart the engine. Follow an appropriate emergency checklist and attempt to determine the cause of the power failure.

- Initially make a quick check for obvious problems.

- Perform restart tasks from memory. Be methodical and troubleshoot in a definite sequence.

- If time permits, refer to the emergency checklist in the AFM/POH.

Using a flow pattern (if practical for your airplane) helps you to remember emergency checklist tasks, such as checking the fuel selector, enriching the mixture, and turning on the auxiliary fuel pump.

When attempting to restart the engine, you normally will not need to use the starter because the propeller usually continues to turn, or windmill, in a power-off glide.

(5) Set up the approach to the emergency landing site.

- Attempt to maneuver the airplane to be at the 180° position on downwind when you reach a normal traffic pattern altitude. From this point, you can perform a normal power-off approach.

If the altitude at which the power failure occurs is too low or the distance to a suitable landing field is too great, you might not be able to arrive at the 180° position. If this situation occurs, plan the approach so the airplane can intercept the normal traffic pattern. For example, the next best place to enter the pattern might be the key position. Keep in mind the distance traveled in the landing flare. If the desired landing point is just beyond a ditch, the aiming point must be on the near side of the ditch.

- If time permits, declare an emergency on 121.5 or the ATC frequency in use—providing your position as accurately as possible. In addition, set your transponder to the emergency code of 7700.

Configure the aircraft for an emergency landing. When the landing is assured, perform the steps outlined in the AFM/POH checklist to configure the airplane and shut down systems to reduce the risk of a post-crash fire. During practice, your instructor might ask you to simulate performing these steps. Depending on the airplane, tasks might include:

- Shut down the engine by moving the fuel selector to OFF, setting the mixture to LEAN (IDLE-CUT-OFF), and turning off the ignition switch.

- Extend the flaps and landing gear (if applicable) as per the AFM/POH.

> Because the flaps shorten the glide distance, do not lower the flaps until you are confident of reaching the emergency landing field.
>
> In rugged terrain and trees, or during impacts at high sink rate, extended gear can protect the cabin area. However, you must weight this factor against the possible side effects of hazards, such as flipping the airplane or collapsing gear rupturing a fuel tank. Consider that a gear-up landing on level, but soft terrain or across a plowed field might result in less risk of injury and airplane damage than a gear-down landing.

- Turn off the master switch.

 Perform the landing. In an actual emergency landing, touch down on the main wheels first. Apply back pressure to hold the nosewheel off the surface for long as possible and then gently lower the nosewheel. Apply the brakes as required to stop the airplane. During a practice emergency landing, initiate a go-around when your instructor directs you to.

ENGINE FAILURE AFTER TAKEOFF

If an engine failure occurs immediately after takeoff before you have reached a safe maneuvering altitude, do not attempt to turn back to the runway. Immediately establish the proper glide attitude and select a field directly ahead or slightly to either side of the takeoff path.

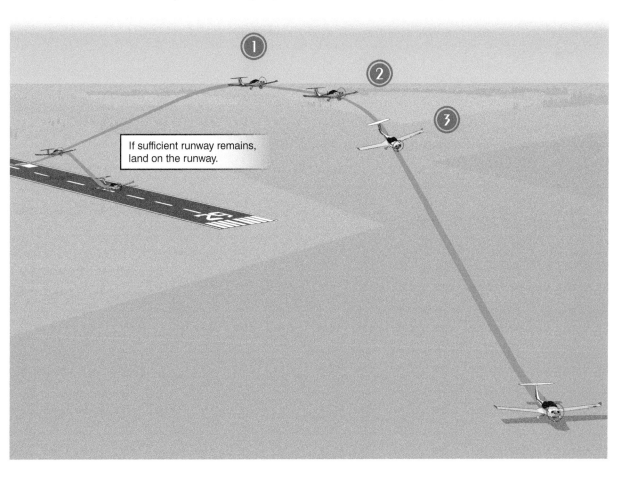

If sufficient runway remains, land on the runway.

MANEUVER 19 ■ Emergency Approach and Landing

Reduce the pitch attitude. Lower the nose and pitch for best glide speed.

> When you practice simulated engine failures at the takeoff climb attitude in the practice area at a safe altitude, you can see how rapidly airspeed decays and why you must immediately pitch down to the attitude for best glide speed.

 If time permits, follow the steps on the emergency checklist. You might have time to perform memory tasks to restart the engine, such as enriching the mixture or turning on the auxiliary fuel pump. However, your focus should be on landing the airplane safely.

 Land straight ahead. Extend the flaps as necessary. Make only small heading changes to avoid obstacles.

> Avoid excessive maneuvering. Continuing straight ahead or making a slight turn allows you more time to establish a safe landing attitude while under control.

An attempt to turn back to the runway in the event of an engine failure after takeoff greatly increases your risk of an accident. Although you might think that a steep turn increases your chances of reaching the runway, steep turns increase the descent rate and stall speed, which is particularly dangerous at slow speeds close to the ground. You also risk a cross-control stall situation if you add excessive rudder to increase the turn rate and add aileron control in the opposite direction to counter the increasing bank angle. See Chapter 5, Maneuver 23 — Demonstrated Stalls for more information regarding cross-control stalls.

A primary risk factor involved with turning back to the runway is insufficient altitude to complete a turn considering the radius and rate of descent. At a safe altitude in the practice area, your instructor might demonstrate an attempt to turn back after simulating an engine failure in the takeoff climb attitude. This demonstration will show you how much altitude is lost during such an attempt in your specific airplane. Consider the altitude loss in the following example.

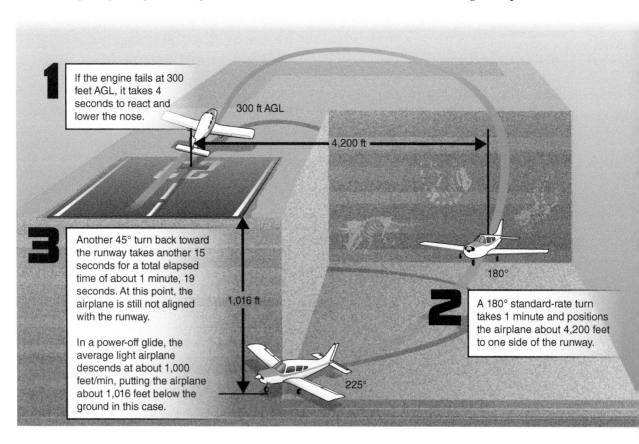

1 If the engine fails at 300 feet AGL, it takes 4 seconds to react and lower the nose.

300 ft AGL

4,200 ft

2 A 180° standard-rate turn takes 1 minute and positions the airplane about 4,200 feet to one side of the runway.

180°

225°

3 Another 45° turn back toward the runway takes another 15 seconds for a total elapsed time of about 1 minute, 19 seconds. At this point, the airplane is still not aligned with the runway.

In a power-off glide, the average light airplane descends at about 1,000 feet/min, putting the airplane about 1,016 feet below the ground in this case.

1,016 ft

MANEUVER 19 ■ Emergency Approach and Landing

ACS

IX. Emergency Operations

Task	B. *Emergency Approach and Landing (Simulated) (ASEL, ASES)*
References	FAA-H-8083-2, FAA-H-8083-3; POH/AFM
Objective	To determine that the applicant exhibits satisfactory knowledge, risk management, and skills associated with emergency approach and landing procedures. ***Note:*** See *Appendix 6: Safety of Flight*.
Knowledge	The applicant demonstrates understanding of:
PA.IX.B.K1	Immediate action items and emergency procedures.
PA.IX.B.K2	Airspeed, to include:
PA.IX.B.K2a	a. Importance of best glide speed and its relationship to distance
PA.IX.B.K2b	b. Difference between best glide speed and minimum sink speed
PA.IX.B.K2c	c. Effects of wind on glide distance
PA.IX.B.K3	Effects of atmospheric conditions on emergency approach and landing.
PA.IX.B.K4	A stabilized approach, to include energy management concepts.
PA.IX.B.K5	ELTs and other emergency locating devices.
PA.IX.B.K6	ATC services to aircraft in distress.
Risk Management	The applicant demonstrates the ability to identify, assess, and mitigate risks, encompassing:
PA.IX.B.R1	Failure to consider altitude, wind, terrain, obstructions, gliding distance, and available landing distance.
PA.IX.B.R2	Failure to plan and follow a flightpath to the selected landing area.
PA.IX.B.R3	Collision hazards, to include aircraft, terrain, obstacles, and wires.
PA.IX.B.R4	Improper airplane configuration.
PA.IX.B.R5	Low altitude maneuvering including stall, spin, or CFIT.
PA.IX.B.R6	Distractions, loss of situational awareness, and/or improper task management.
Skills	The applicant demonstrates the ability to:
PA.IX.B.S1	Establish and maintain the recommended best glide airspeed, ±10 knots.
PA.IX.B.S2	Configure the airplane in accordance with the POH/AFM and existing conditions.
PA.IX.B.S3	Select a suitable landing area considering altitude, wind, terrain, obstructions, and available glide distance.
PA.IX.B.S4	Plan and follow a flightpath to the selected landing area considering altitude, wind, terrain, and obstructions.
PA.IX.B.S5	Prepare for landing as specified by the evaluator.
PA.IX.B.S6	Complete the appropriate checklist.

MANEUVER 19 ■ **Emergency Approach and Landing**

MANEUVER 19 ■ **Emergency Approach and Landing**

EXERCISES — EMERGENCY OPERATIONS

17 — SYSTEMS AND EQUIPMENT MALFUNCTIONS

1. What actions should you take if you experience a partial power loss?

_____

_____

_____

2. What actions should you take if the alternator fails?

_____

_____

_____

3. What are three factors to consider when performing a no-flap approach and landing?

_____

_____

_____

4. What actions should you take to manage smoke or fire in the cabin?

_____

_____

_____

5. What should you do if a door opens in flight?

_____

18 — EMERGENCY DESCENT

1. What is the purpose of an emergency descent?

_____

2. You are performing an emergency descent with full flaps in smooth conditions. What is the airspeed limitation for the descent?
    A. V_A
    B. V_{NE}
    C. V_{FE}

3. What are two reasons to perform an emergency descent in a turn?

_____

_____

EXERCISES   Emergency Operations

4. In turbulent air, at what airspeed would you perform an emergency descent if the airplane had no flaps or landing gear extended? _____

5. During a 1000 ft/min descent, you plan to at 3,000 feet MSL. At what altitude should you begin your leveloff? _____

19 — EMERGENCY APPROACH AND LANDING

1. What is the first action you should take when an engine failure occurs?

   _____

2. True/False. You should perform the engine failure checklist as a do-list.

3. Name at least two factors that you need to consider when selecting an appropriate field for an emergency landing.

   _____

4. True/False. When making an emergency landing, it is recommended that you circle away from the field and perform a long straight-in approach to the landing area.

5. What code should you set in your transponder to indicate an emergency? _____

6. Why should you wait to extend the flaps until you are confident of making the landing field?

   _____

7. What are the three steps to follow if an engine failure occurs immediately after takeoff before you have reached a safe maneuvering altitude and sufficient runway is not available?

   _____

   _____

   _____

8. Why does an attempt to turn back to the runway in the event of an engine failure after takeoff greatly increase your risk of an accident?

   _____

   _____

   _____

CHAPTER 5

Flight Maneuvers

COLLISION AVOIDANCE/CLEARING TURNS

Collision avoidance is an important safety consideration every time you fly and particularly when maneuvering your airplane in the practice area. In the practice environment you can be easily distracted so you should make a special effort to maintain your visual scan while maneuvering. Your instructor will help you with your scanning technique and encourage you to concentrate your vision outside the airplane. Your instructor also will show you how to clear the area prior to maneuvering.

Before you begin a maneuver, you should make clearing turns that usually consist of at least a 180° change in direction, such as two 90° turns. Clearing turns provide you with a view of the area around your flight path and make it easier to maintain visual contact with other aircraft in the practice area.

20 — Slow Flight

The purpose of maneuvering during slow flight is to help you develop a feel for the airplane's controls at slow airspeeds, as well as to understand how load factor, pitch attitude, airspeed, and altitude control relate to each other. Slow flight can be broadly defined as flight at an airspeed below the normal cruise speed. However, during training you will normally practice this maneuver at airspeeds well below the normal cruise speed. For the practical test, the *Private Pilot Airman Certification Standards (ACS)* state that you should "establish and maintain an airspeed at which any further increase in angle of attack, increase in load factor, or reduction in power would result in a stall warning (e.g. aircraft buffet, stall horn, etc.)." The following discussion describes performing slow flight according to the ACS definition.

While in slow flight, any change in flight attitude, such as a level turn or increase in pitch attitude, increases the airplane's load factor and its stall speed. Because the airspeed is just above a stall speed during slow flight, you typically must add power to prevent the airplane from stalling during maneuvering. Coordinated flight is essential throughout all slow flight maneuvers.

Slow flight is typically performed and evaluated in the landing configuration with flaps and landing gear (if applicable) extended. However, performing slow flight in a clean configuration or with partial flaps is good practice and can be evaluated on the practical test. Before beginning slow flight, perform clearing turns to check for traffic—one 180° turn or two 90° turns in opposite directions. Start the maneuver at an altitude that enables you to recover no lower than 1,500 feet AGL. Select an entry altitude and heading that you can easily read on the instruments, such as 3,500 feet and 090°.

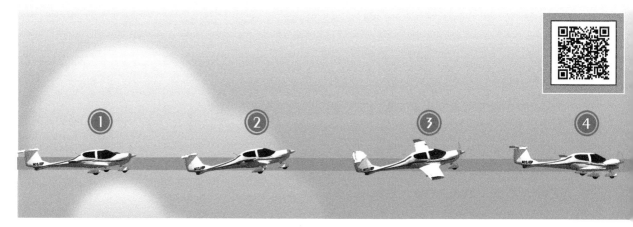

① **Decrease the airspeed.** After completing clearing turns, apply carburetor heat (if applicable), reduce power, and gradually apply back pressure on the control stick to maintain altitude. Use the rudder pedals to stay on heading and maintain coordinated flight. Trim to relieve control pressures.

② **Stabilize at the desired airspeed.**

- When the airplane slows below maximum flaps extended speed (V_{FE}), lower the flaps in increments. As the flaps extend, adjust the pitch attitude and power to maintain altitude. Extend the landing gear (if applicable) after slowing to V_{LE}. Trim to relieve control pressures after each configuration change.

- Upon reaching your desired airspeed, increase power to maintain altitude and apply right rudder to counteract the left-turning tendency.

> The forces of torque, P-factor, gyroscopic precession, and spiraling slipstream create a left-turning tendency during flight with a low airspeed, high angle of attack, and high power setting.

After established in slow flight, primarily maintain airspeed and altitude by making small power adjustments as necessary. To maintain the proper pitch attitude, divide your attention between outside references and instrument indications. The correct procedure for regaining lost altitude is to apply power and make a small increase in pitch attitude to maintain the desired airspeed. To lose altitude, reduce power and, at the same time, reduce pitch attitude slightly.

 Perform climbs, descents, and turns. After the airplane is stabilized, perform these maneuvers as directed by your instructor.

- To climb, increase pitch and add power to maintain airspeed. Correspondingly, to descend, decrease both pitch and reduce power to maintain airspeed.

- To perform a turn, add power to maintain airspeed and avoid a stall. Limit the bank angle to 20°.

When you are maneuvering during slow flight, you will get a sensation of insufficient control response. The controls feel mushy, and you must use greater control movements for corrections than are normally required.

 Return to cruise flight.

- Apply forward pressure on the control stick, add full power, and set the carburetor heat to COLD (if applicable).

- Retract the flaps slowly in increments. Also, retract the landing gear (if applicable).

- Reduce right rudder pressure as the airplane accelerates. When you reach your desired airspeed, reduce power and trim to relieve control pressures.

MANEUVER 18 ■ **Slow Flight**

VII. Slow Flight and Stalls

Task	A. Maneuvering During Slow Flight
References	FAA-H-8083-2, FAA-H-8083-3; POH/AFM
Objective	To determine that the applicant exhibits satisfactory knowledge, risk management, and skills associated with maneuvering during slow flight. **Note:** See Appendix 6: Safety of Flight and Appendix 7: Aircraft, Equipment, and Operational Requirements & Limitations.
Knowledge	The applicant demonstrates understanding of:
PA.VII.A.K1	Aerodynamics associated with slow flight in various airplane configurations, to include the relationship between angle of attack, airspeed, load factor, power setting, airplane weight and center of gravity, airplane attitude, and yaw effects.
Risk Management	The applicant demonstrates the ability to identify, assess and mitigate risks, encompassing:
PA.VII.A.R1	Inadvertent slow flight and flight with a stall warning, which could lead to loss of control.
PA.VII.A.R2	Range and limitations of stall warning indicators (e.g., airplane buffet, stall horn, etc.).
PA.VII.A.R3	Failure to maintain coordinated flight.
PA.VII.A.R4	Effect of environmental elements on airplane performance (e.g., turbulence, microbursts, and high-density altitude).
PA.VII.A.R5	Collision hazards, to include aircraft, terrain, obstacles, and wires.
PA.VII.A.R6	Distractions, loss of situational awareness, and/or improper task management.
Skills	The applicant demonstrates the ability to:
PA.VII.A.S1	Clear the area.
PA.VII.A.S2	Select an entry altitude that will allow the Task to be completed no lower than 1,500 feet AGL (ASEL, ASES) or 3,000 feet AGL (AMEL, AMES).
PA.VII.A.S3	Establish and maintain an airspeed at which any further increase in angle of attack, increase in load factor, or reduction in power, would result in a stall warning (e.g., airplane buffet, stall horn, etc.).
PA.VII.A.S4	Accomplish coordinated straight-and-level flight, turns, climbs, and descents with the airplane configured as specified by the evaluator without a stall warning (e.g., airplane buffet, stall horn, etc.).
PA.VII.A.S5	Maintain the specified altitude, ±100 feet; specified heading, ±10°; airspeed, +10/-0 knots; and specified angle of bank, ±10°.

21 — Power-Off Stalls

Both the regulations for private pilot certification and the ACS require that students are able to enter and perform stalls. You are not required to demonstrate flight proficiency in spins. However, you must have aeronautical knowledge training in stall awareness, spin entry, spins, and spin recovery techniques. In addition, according to the ACS, your knowledge of the aerodynamics associated with stalls in various aircraft configurations can be evaluated during the practical test. These aerodynamic subjects include the relationship between angle of attack, airspeed, load factor, power setting, aircraft weight and center of gravity, aircraft attitude, and yaw effects. A thorough discussion of these topics is contained in Jeppesen *Private Pilot* textbook.

STALL CHARACTERISTICS

Practicing intentional stalls will familiarize you with the conditions that result in a stall, enable you to recognize an impending stall, and help you develop the proper corrective response if a stall occurs. You should understand the possible flight scenarios in which an inadvertent stall could occur. For example, a power-off turning stall could develop if the controls are improperly used during a turn from the base leg to the final approach. A power-off straight-ahead stall could occur when trying to stretch a glide after the engine has failed, or if low on the approach to landing. According to the ACS, for the practical test you are expected to acknowledge the cues of an impending stall and then recover promptly after a full stall has occurred.

- Impending stall—a buffet or aural warning is triggered but the wings have not reached the critical angle of attack.

- Full stall—the critical angle of attack is exceeded. Indications of a full stall are typically an uncommanded nose-down pitch that can be combined with an uncommanded rolling motion.

You typically perform power-off stalls in the landing configuration to simulate an inadvertent stall during approach. As the airplane approaches a stall, the control feel is sometimes described as "mushy" or "soft" as compared to the more solid feel of the controls at cruise speed. Consequently, you must apply more control pressure to achieve the desired results. As the airplane slows you also will notice a decrease in engine sound and slipstream noise. The airplane's mechanical stall warning, which may be a light, buzzer, horn, or other device, usually begins 5 to 10 knots before the stall. You might notice buffeting and further decay of control effectiveness just before the stall.

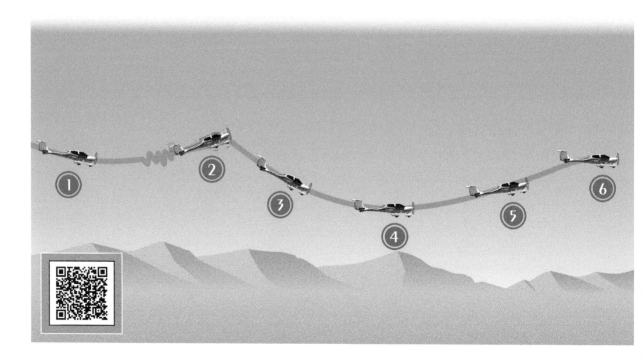

STRAIGHT-AHEAD STALL

Before you begin setting up the stall, you should perform clearing turns and establish the airplane at an altitude which will allow you to recover by 1,500 feet AGL.

 Establish a glide.

- After completing clearing turns, apply carburetor heat (if applicable), reduce power to idle (or normal approach power), and gradually apply back pressure on the control stick to maintain altitude.

- As you reach the safe flap extension speed, lower the flaps in increments and establish a normal glide. Extend the landing gear (if applicable). Trim to relieve control pressures.

Practice power-off stalls at all flap settings to simulate a variety of conditions under which an inadvertent stall could occur.

 Induce the stall. Maintain coordinated flight using the rudder pedals and apply back pressure on the control stick to raise the airplane's nose to an attitude that will induce a stall. Maintain the pitch attitude until a full stall occurs.

Do not carry airspeed in excess of the normal approach speed into the stall entry. Excess airspeed can cause an abnormally nose-high attitude.

 Recover from the stall. Release back pressure to reduce the angle of attack. Level the wings (if necessary) using coordinated aileron and rudder pressure. Add full power, and set the carburetor heat to COLD (if applicable). Retract the flaps to an intermediate setting.

You might need right rudder pressure to overcome the engine torque effects as you apply power and lower the nose.

 Stop the descent. As airspeed is regained, gently pull back on the control stick to stop the descent and initiate a climb.

Ensure you apply the correct amount of back pressure during stall recoveries. Applying back pressure too rapidly can cause a secondary stall, while not applying it quickly enough can cause the airplane to build excessive airspeed and lose a significant amount of altitude.

 Establish a climb. After you establish a positive rate of climb, retract the landing gear (if applicable). Upon reaching V_X or V_Y, retract the remainder of the flaps. Trim to relieve control pressures.

 Return to straight-and-level flight. Upon reaching the desired altitude, level off and accelerate to the desired airspeed. Return to the proper heading, if necessary. After you attain the proper airspeed, adjust the power and trim to relieve control pressures.

MANEUVER 19 ■ **Power-Off Stalls**

TURNING STALL

The power-off, turning stall—a variation of the power-off straight-ahead stall—is designed to simulate an inadvertent stall during a turn from base to final. Entry procedures are the same as the straight-ahead, power-off stall except with the addition of up to a 20° angle of bank.

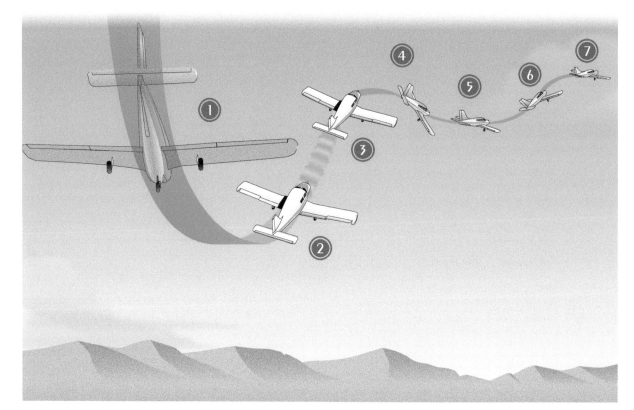

MANEUVER 19 ■ **Power-Off Stalls**

① Establish a glide.

- After completing clearing turns, apply carburetor heat (if applicable), reduce power to idle (or normal approach power), and gradually apply back pressure on the control wheel to maintain altitude.

- As you reach the safe flap extension speed, lower the flaps in increments and establish a normal glide. Extend the landing gear (if applicable). Trim to relieve control pressures.

② Enter a turn. Begin a shallow-banked turn to the left or right (up to 20° bank angle). After you are established in the turn, maintain coordinated flight and apply back pressure on the control wheel to raise the airplane's nose to an attitude that will induce a stall.

③ Induce the stall. Maintain the desired angle of bank in coordinated flight using the rudder pedals. Maintain the pitch attitude until a full stall occurs.

> Do not attempt to stall or recover on a particular heading. However, to simulate the turn from base to final, induce the stall within 90° of turn.
>
> It is critical to maintain coordinated flight during all stalls, particularly those that incorporate a turn. If not in coordinated flight during a turning, power-off stall, the airplane can wallow when the stall occurs or, if the airplane is in a slip, the outer wing can stall first and abruptly move downward.

④ Recover from the stall. Release back pressure to reduce the angle of attack. Level the wings using coordinated aileron and rudder pressure. Add full power, and set the carburetor heat to COLD (if applicable). Retract the flaps to an intermediate setting.

(5) Stop the descent. As airspeed is regained, gently pull back on the control wheel to stop the descent and initiate a climb.

Ensure you apply the correct amount of back pressure during stall recoveries. Applying back pressure too rapidly can cause a secondary stall, while not applying it quickly enough can cause the airplane to build excessive airspeed and lose a significant amount of altitude.

(6) Establish a climb. After you establish a positive rate of climb, retract the landing gear (if applicable). Upon reaching V_X or V_Y, retract the remainder of the flaps. Trim to relieve control pressures.

(7) Return to straight-and-level flight. Upon reaching the desired altitude, level off and accelerate to the desired airspeed. Return to the proper heading, if necessary. After you attain the proper airspeed, adjust the power and trim to relieve control pressures.

MANEUVER 19 ▪ Power-Off Stalls

VII. Slow Flight and Stalls

Task	B. Power-Off Stalls
References	FAA-H-8083-2, FAA-H-8083-3; AC 61-67; POH/AFM
Objective	To determine that the applicant exhibits satisfactory knowledge, risk management, and skills associated with power-off stalls. **Note:** See _Appendix 7: Aircraft, Equipment, and Operational Requirements & Limitations_.
Knowledge	The applicant demonstrates understanding of:
PA.VII.B.K1	Aerodynamics associated with stalls in various airplane configurations, to include the relationship between angle of attack, airspeed, load factor, power setting, airplane weight and center of gravity, airplane attitude, and yaw effects.
PA.VII.B.K2	Stall characteristics (i.e., airplane design) and impending stall and full stall indications (i.e., how to recognize by sight, sound, or feel).
PA.VII.B.K3	Factors and situations that can lead to a power-off stall and actions that can be taken to prevent it.
PA.VII.B.K4	Fundamentals of stall recovery.
Risk Management	The applicant demonstrates the ability to identify, assess and mitigate risks, encompassing:
PA.VII.B.R1	Factors and situations that could lead to an inadvertent power-off stall, spin, and loss of control.
PA.VII.B.R2	Range and limitations of stall warning indicators (e.g., airplane buffet, stall horn, etc.).
PA.VII.B.R3	Failure to recognize and recover at the stall warning during normal operations.
PA.VII.B.R4	Improper stall recovery procedure.
PA.VII.B.R5	Secondary stalls, accelerated stalls, and cross-control stalls.
PA.VII.B.R6	Effect of environmental elements on airplane performance related to power-off stalls (e.g., turbulence, microbursts, and high-density altitude).
PA.VII.B.R7	Collision hazards, to include airplane, terrain, obstacles, and wires.
PA.VII.B.R8	Distractions, loss of situational awareness, and/or improper task management.
Skills	The applicant demonstrates the ability to:
PA.VII.B.S1	Clear the area.
PA.VII.B.S2	Select an entry altitude that will allow the Task to be completed no lower than 1,500 feet AGL (ASEL, ASES) or 3,000 feet AGL (AMEL, AMES).
PA.VII.B.S3	Configure the airplane in the approach or landing configuration, as specified by the evaluator, and maintain coordinated flight throughout the maneuver.
PA.VII.B.S4	Establish a stabilized descent.
PA.VII.B.S5	Transition smoothly from the approach or landing attitude to a pitch attitude that will induce a stall.
PA.VII.B.S6	Maintain a specified heading, ±10° if in straight flight; maintain a specified angle of bank not to exceed 20°, ±10°, if in turning flight, while inducing the stall.
PA.VII.B.S7	Acknowledge cues of the impending stall and then recover promptly after a full stall occurs.
PA.VII.B.S8	Execute a stall recovery in accordance with procedures set forth in the POH/AFM.
PA.VII.B.S9	Configure the airplane as recommended by the manufacturer, and accelerate to V_X or V_Y.
PA.VII.B.S10	Return to the altitude, heading, and airspeed specified by the evaluator.

22 — Power-On Stalls

You usually practice power-on stalls from straight climbs and climbing turns to simulate an inadvertent stall during takeoffs, go-arounds, climbs, or when trying to clear an obstacle. Applying excessive back pressure in one of these situations produces an extreme nose-high attitude and high angle of attack. The power-on, turning stall can occur during the departure turn following takeoff and is caused by distractions that divert your attention from flying the airplane or by attempting to clear obstacles or rising terrain.

The indications of an impending or full stall are similar to those you experience during a power-off stall (see Maneuver 21 — Power-Off Stalls). Practice power-on stalls at an entry altitude that permits a safe recovery no lower than 1,500 feet AGL and in the takeoff/departure configuration at the aircraft's takeoff speed. Depending on the airplane, you might have the landing gear and/or takeoff flaps extended.

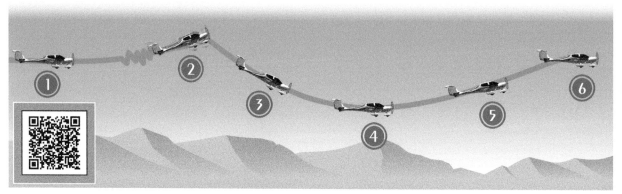

STRAIGHT-AHEAD STALL

Although you use a high power setting during this stall, do not enter it from a high airspeed. A high-power, high-airspeed stall entry can cause an extremely nose-high pitch attitude.

① **Slow to takeoff speed.** After completing clearing turns, reduce power and slow the airplane while using back pressure on the control stick to maintain altitude.

② **Induce the stall.** As you reach liftoff speed, simultaneously set takeoff power (or the recommended climb power setting) and smoothly apply back pressure on the control stick to raise the airplane's nose to an attitude that will induce a stall. Maintain the pitch attitude until a full stall occurs. Ensure you maintain coordinated flight.

> You will need increasing right rudder pressure to maintain coordinated flight as you increase the power and pitch attitude.

③ **Recover from the stall.** Simultaneously release back pressure and apply full power (if not already at full power). If you lowered flaps, retract them to an intermediate setting.

> As the nose pitches down, the airplane might roll to one side. If this occurs, use coordinated aileron and rudder pressures to level the wings.
>
> You might use a takeoff flap setting during power-on stalls. In that case, you will wait to retract the flaps until achieving a positive rate of climb.

④ **Stop the descent.** As airspeed is regained, gently pull back on the control stick to stop the descent and initiate a climb.

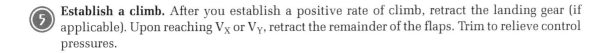

Applying the correct amount of back pressure during stall recoveries is essential. Applying back pressure too rapidly can cause a secondary stall. Not applying back pressure quickly enough can cause the airplane to build excessive airspeed and lose a significant amount of altitude.

(5) Establish a climb. After you establish a positive rate of climb, retract the landing gear (if applicable). Upon reaching V_X or V_Y, retract the remainder of the flaps. Trim to relieve control pressures.

(6) Return to straight-and-level flight. Upon reaching the desired altitude, level off and accelerate to the desired airspeed. Return to the proper heading, if necessary. After you attain the proper airspeed, adjust the power and trim to relieve control pressures.

TURNING STALL

The power-on, turning stall is a variation of the power-on straight-ahead stall. Entry procedures are the same as the straight-ahead, power-on stall except with the addition of up to a 20° angle of bank.

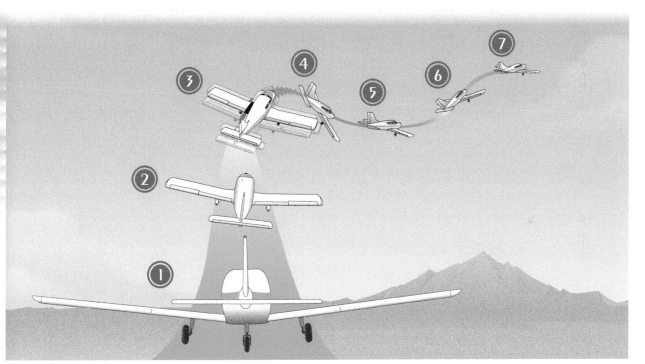

(1) Slow to takeoff speed. After completing clearing turns, reduce power and slow the airplane while using back pressure on the control wheel to maintain altitude.

(2) Enter a turn. As you approach liftoff speed, begin a shallow-banked turn to the left or right (up to 20° bank angle).

(3) Induce the stall. Upon reaching liftoff speed, simultaneously set takeoff power (or the recommended climb power setting) and smoothly apply back pressure on the control stick to raise the airplane's nose to an attitude that will induce a stall. Ensure you maintain the desired angle of bank and coordinated flight.

Because torque and P-factor tend to roll the airplane to the left, as you approach the stall, the angle of bank tends to steepen in a left turn and become shallower in a right turn.

Do not attempt to stall or recover on a particular heading but try to induce the stall within 90° of turn.

④ Recover from the stall. Simultaneously release back pressure, roll wings-level using coordinated rudder and aileron pressure, and apply full power (if not already at full power). If you lowered takeoff flaps, retract them.

④ Stop the descent. As airspeed is regained, adjust the pitch attitude to stop the descent and initiate a climb.

> Applying the correct amount of back pressure during stall recoveries is essential. Applying back pressure too rapidly can cause a secondary stall. Not applying back pressure quickly enough can cause the airplane to build excessive airspeed and lose a significant amount of altitude.

⑤ Establish a climb. After you establish a positive rate of climb, retract the landing gear (if applicable). Upon reaching V_X or V_Y, retract the remainder of the flaps. Trim to relieve control pressures.

⑥ Return to straight-and-level flight. After reaching the desired altitude, level off and accelerate to the desired airspeed. Return to the proper heading, if necessary. After you attain the proper airspeed, adjust the power and trim to relieve control pressures.

VII. Slow Flight and Stalls

Task	C. Power-On Stalls
References	FAA-H-8083-2, FAA-H-8083-3; AC 61-67; POH/AFM
Objective	To determine that the applicant exhibits satisfactory knowledge, risk management, and skills associated with power-on stalls. **Note:** See _Appendix 6: Safety of Flight_ and _Appendix 7: Aircraft, Equipment, and Operational Requirements & Limitations_.
Knowledge	The applicant demonstrates understanding of:
PA.VII.C.K1	Aerodynamics associated with stalls in various airplane configurations, to include the relationship between angle of attack, airspeed, load factor, power setting, airplane weight and center of gravity, airplane attitude, and yaw effects.
PA.VII.C.K2	Stall characteristics (i.e., airplane design) and impending stall and full stall indications (i.e., how to recognize by sight, sound, or feel).
PA.VII.C.K3	Factors and situations that can lead to a power-on stall and actions that can be taken to prevent it.
PA.VII.C.K4	Fundamentals of stall recovery.
Risk Management	The applicant demonstrates the ability to identify, assess and mitigate risks, encompassing:
PA.VII.C.R1	Factors and situations that could lead to an inadvertent power-on stall, spin, and loss of control.
PA.VII.C.R2	Range and limitations of stall warning indicators (e.g., airplane buffet, stall horn, etc.).
PA.VII.C.R3	Failure to recognize and recover at the stall warning during normal operations.
PA.VII.C.R4	Improper stall recovery procedure.
PA.VII.C.R5	Secondary stalls, accelerated stalls, elevator trim stalls, and cross-control stalls.
PA.VII.C.R6	Effect of environmental elements on airplane performance related to power-on stalls (e.g., turbulence, microbursts, and high-density altitude).
PA.VII.C.R7	Collision hazards, to include aircraft, terrain, obstacles, and wires.
PA.VII.C.R8	Distractions, loss of situational awareness, and/or improper task management.
Skills	The applicant demonstrates the ability to:
PA.VII.C.S1	Clear the area.
PA.VII.C.S2	Select an entry altitude that will allow the Task to be completed no lower than 1,500 feet AGL (ASEL, ASES) or 3,000 feet AGL (AMEL, AMES).
PA.VII.C.S3	Establish the takeoff, departure, or cruise configuration, as specified by the evaluator, and maintain coordinated flight throughout the maneuver.
PA.VII.C.S4	Set power (as assigned by the evaluator) to no less than 65 percent available power.
PA.VII.C.S5	Transition smoothly from the takeoff or departure attitude to the pitch attitude that will induce a stall.
PA.VII.C.S6	Maintain a specified heading, ±10° if in straight flight; maintain a specified angle of bank not to exceed 20°, ±10° if in turning flight, while inducing the stall.
PA.VII.C.S7	Acknowledge cues of the impending stall and then recover promptly after a full stall occurs.
PA.VII.C.S8	Execute a stall recovery in accordance with procedures set forth in the POH/AFM.
PA.VII.C.S9	Configure the airplane as recommended by the manufacturer, and accelerate to V_X or V_Y.
PA.VII.C.S10	Return to the altitude, heading, and airspeed specified by the evaluator.

MANEUVER 20 ▪ **Power-On Stalls**

23 — Demonstrated Stalls and Spin Awareness

The ACS require that an applicant for the practical test demonstrates the ability to identify, assess and mitigate risks regarding secondary stalls, accelerated stalls, elevator trim stalls, and cross-control stalls. However, although you are required to demonstrate your ability to perform power-off and power-on stalls for the practical test, secondary, accelerated maneuver stalls, cross-control stalls, and elevator trim stalls may only be demonstrated by your instructor and only if your airplane is certificated for these types of operations. The procedures contained in the following discussion are presented so you can more completely understand how and why the stalls occur and how the associated recovery should be accomplished. Do not practice these maneuvers during solo flight.

For each type of demonstrated stall, you should be able to recognize the stall cause and characteristics and learn the correct recovery methods. After clearing turns, your instructor will demonstrate the stall at an altitude that ensures a safe recovery no lower than 1,500 feet AGL.

SECONDARY STALLS

A secondary stall is caused by trying to recover from a stall before the airplane has obtained sufficient flying speed. This type of stall can also occur if you attempt to return to straight-and-level flight prematurely during a spin recovery. After clearing turns, your instructor will start the demonstration using the listed procedures at an altitude that will ensure a safe recovery no lower than 1,500 feet AGL.

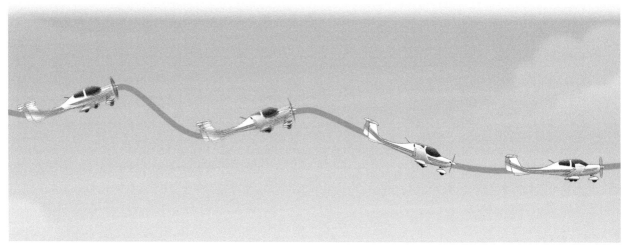

Secondary Stall Cause
You pitch up too quickly during a stall recovery before the airplane reaches sufficient flying speed.

Secondary Stall Demonstration
Perform a normal power-on or power-off stall and during recovery, quickly increase the pitch attitude again while maintaining directional control with aileron and rudder pressure. Allow the airplane to enter the secondary stall.

Secondary Stall Recovery
Release back pressure on the control stick to reduce the angle of attack and ensure full power is set. Stop the descent by gently pulling back on the control stick.

ACCELERATED STALL

An accelerated stall occurs at a higher-than-normal airspeed in steep turns, pullups, or other abrupt changes in flight attitude. The stalls that occur from these types of maneuvers tend to develop faster than normal unaccelerated stalls. It is important to recover at the first indication of the stall. A prolonged stall, with excessive airspeed can lead to a spin.

Accelerated Stall Cause
You impose high maneuvering loads by using excessive back pressure in steep turns, pull-ups, or other abrupt changes in attitude, causing a stall at a higher-than-normal airspeed.

Accelerated Stall Demonstration
Establish straight-and-level flight at V_A or less. Roll into a 45° angle of bank level turn while gradually increasing back pressure to maintain altitude. After the turn and bank are established, slowly increase back pressure while maintaining altitude until the airplane stalls.

Accelerated Stall Recovery
Immediately release the back pressure on the control stick and add power. To prevent one wing from dropping suddenly, use coordinated aileron and rudder pressure to return to straight-and-level flight.

CROSS-CONTROL STALLS

A cross-control stall is most likely to occur in the traffic pattern during a turn from the base leg to final approach when trying to compensate for overshooting the extended runway centerline. The following scenario describes how this can happen.

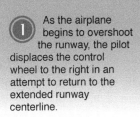
1. As the airplane begins to overshoot the runway, the pilot displaces the control wheel to the right in an attempt to return to the extended runway centerline.

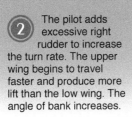
2. The pilot adds excessive right rudder to increase the turn rate. The upper wing begins to travel faster and produce more lift than the low wing. The angle of bank increases.

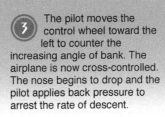
3. The pilot moves the control wheel toward the left to counter the increasing angle of bank. The airplane is now cross-controlled. The nose begins to drop and the pilot applies back pressure to arrest the rate of descent.

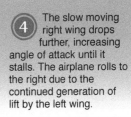
4. The slow moving right wing drops further, increasing angle of attack until it stalls. The airplane rolls to the right due to the continued generation of lift by the left wing.

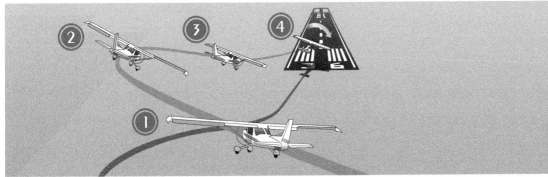

MANEUVER 21 ■ **Demonstrated Stalls**

In a cross-control stall, the airplane often stalls with little warning. The nose can pitch down, the inside wing can suddenly drop, and the airplane can continue to roll to an inverted attitude. This is usually the beginning of a spin, which is very dangerous at lower altitudes. If a cross-control stall occurs during an actual approach to a landing, recovering safely might be impossible due to the amount of altitude needed.

Cross-Control Stall Cause
You apply aileron pressure in one direction, rudder pressure in the opposite direction, and use excessive elevator/stabilator back pressure.

Cross-Control Stall Demonstration
Slowly reduce power and extend the landing gear (if applicable). Continue reducing the power to idle and maintain altitude until a normal glide speed is reached. Establish a normal glide and trim to relieve control pressures. After the aircraft is established in the descent, roll into a medium bank turn and apply heavy rudder pressure in the direction of the turn. Maintain the bank by applying opposite aileron pressure. As you do so, increase back pressure on the control stick to keep the nose from lowering. Increase all flight control pressures until the airplane stalls.

Cross-Control Stall Recovery
When the stall occurs, release the control pressures. If necessary, allow the roll to continue until the airplane reaches upright and level flight. Increase power to maintain straight-and-level flight.

MANEUVER 21 ■ **Demonstrated Stalls**

ELEVATOR TRIM STALLS

The elevator trim stall is a maneuver that demonstrates what can happen when you apply full power during a go-around and you do not have positive control of the airplane. This type of stall can happen during a normal landing approach, a simulated forced landing approach, or immediately after takeoff. You must immediately recognize the approaching stall and promptly recover to prevent the stall. If a power-on stall occurs from an actual go-around, the amount of pitch change and altitude required for a safe recovery might not be available.

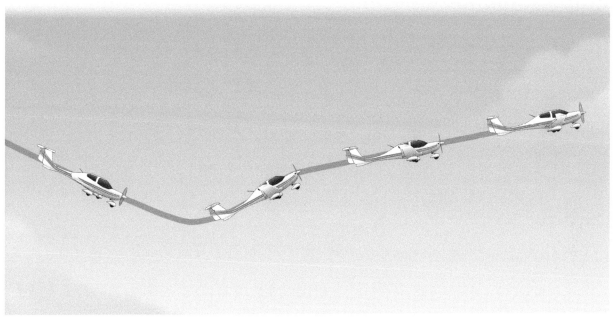

Elevator Trim Stall Cause

You perform a go-around and let the airplane pitch up to a stall attitude because the trim is set for landing, or you perform a takeoff with excessive nose-up trim.

Elevator Trim Stall Demonstration

Slowly reduce power and extend the landing gear (if applicable). Extend 1/2 to full flaps and continue reducing the power to idle. Maintain altitude until the airplane reaches a normal glide speed. Establish a normal glide, trim the nose up to simulate a landing approach, and apply full power to simulate a go-around. The combined forces of power, engine torque, and back elevator/ stabilator trim will make the nose pitch up sharply with a left-turning tendency. As the pitch attitude increases to a point well above the normal climb attitude, the potential for a stall exists.

Impending Elevator Trim Stall Recovery

Before the stall occurs, apply forward pressure on the control stick to return to a normal climb attitude. Trim to relieve control pressure and continue the climb until reaching the desired altitude.

SPIN AWARENESS

As an applicant for a private pilot certificate, you are not required to demonstrate flight proficiency in spin entries, spins, or spin recovery procedures. However, regulatory requirement for every recreational, private, and commercial pilot applicant includes aeronautical knowledge training in stall awareness, spin entry, spins, and spin recovery techniques. The ACS also require that you exhibit satisfactory knowledge, risk management, and skills associated with spins, flight situations where unintentional spins may occur and procedures for recovery from unintentional spins. Your flight instructor might demonstrate a spin sometime during your training—spins should never be attempted without an experienced instructor on board. A thorough discussion of spins is contained in the Jeppesen *Private Pilot* textbook.

MANEUVER 21 ■ **Demonstrated Stalls**

SPIN CONDITIONS

A spin is an aggravated stall that results in autorotation—the airplane descends in a corkscrew path. For an airplane to enter a spin, the wings must stall, the ailerons and rudder must be uncoordinated, and one wing must be more fully stalled than the other wing. In light, training airplanes, a complete spin maneuver consists of three phases—incipient, fully developed, and recovery.

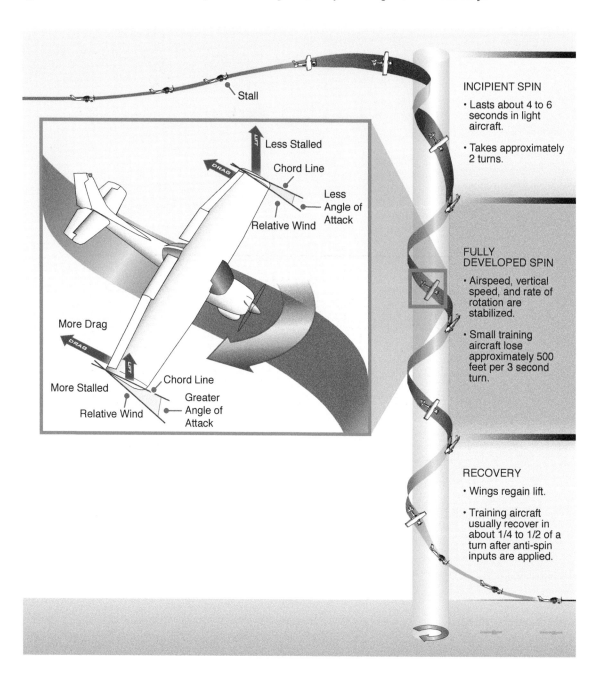

Stall

Less Stalled

Chord Line

Less Angle of Attack

Relative Wind

More Drag

More Stalled

Chord Line

Greater Angle of Attack

Relative Wind

INCIPIENT SPIN

• Lasts about 4 to 6 seconds in light aircraft.

• Takes approximately 2 turns.

FULLY DEVELOPED SPIN

• Airspeed, vertical speed, and rate of rotation are stabilized.

• Small training aircraft lose approximately 500 feet per 3 second turn.

RECOVERY

• Wings regain lift.

• Training aircraft usually recover in about 1/4 to 1/2 of a turn after anti-spin inputs are applied.

SPIN RECOVERY

You must follow the specific spin recovery procedures in your airplane's AFM/POH. If the AFM/POH does not state a procedure, the following general steps are recommended by the FAA.

1. Reduce the power to idle. Moving the throttle to idle will eliminate thrust and minimize the altitude loss.

2. Position the ailerons to neutral.

3. Apply full opposite rudder against the rotation.

4. Apply a positive and brisk straight forward movement of the elevator control forward of neutral to break the stall.

5. After the spin rotation stops, neutralize the rudder.

6. Apply back-elevator pressure to raise the nose to level flight.

VII. Slow Flight and Stalls

Task	D. Spin Awareness
References	FAA-H-8083-2, FAA-H-8083-3; AC 61-67; POH/AFM
Objective	To determine that the applicant exhibits satisfactory knowledge, risk management, and skills associated with spins, flight situations where unintentional spins may occur and procedures for recovery from unintentional spins.
Knowledge	The applicant demonstrates understanding of:
PA.VII.D.K1	Aerodynamics associated with spins in various airplane configurations, to include the relationship between angle of attack, airspeed, load factor, power setting, aircraft weight and center of gravity, aircraft attitude, and yaw effects.
PA.VII.D.K2	What causes a spin and how to identify the entry, incipient, and developed phases of a spin.
PA.VII.D.K3	Spin recovery procedure.
Risk Management	The applicant demonstrates the ability to identify, assess and mitigate risks, encompassing:
PA.VII.D.R1	Factors and situations that could lead to inadvertent spin and loss of control.
PA.VII.D.R2	Range and limitations of stall warning indicators (e.g., airplane buffet, stall horn, etc.).
PA.VII.D.R3	Improper spin recovery procedure.
PA.VII.D.R4	Effect of environmental elements on airplane performance related to spins (e.g., turbulence, microbursts, and high-density altitude).
PA.VII.D.R5	Collision hazards, to include aircraft, terrain, obstacles, and wires.
PA.VII.D.R6	Distractions, loss of situational awareness, and/or improper task management.
Skills	[Intentionally left blank]

MANEUVER 21 ▪ **Demonstrated Stalls**

24 — Steep Turns

A steep turn is a high-performance maneuver that you usually perform in either direction with an angle of bank of 45°, ±5°. Due to high load factors, perform steep turns at an airspeed that does not exceed the airplane's maneuvering speed (V_A). The objective of performing steep turns is to develop smoothness, coordination, orientation, division of attention, and control techniques. As with most flight maneuvers, you should select an entry altitude which will allow you to perform the maneuver no lower than 1,500 feet AGL.

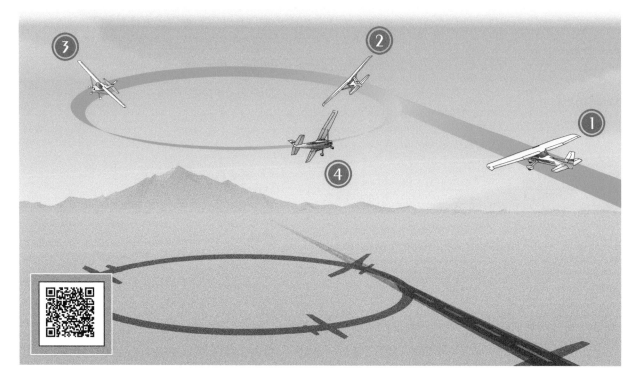

① Establish references and the proper airspeed. After completing clearing turns, select a reference point on the horizon and note your heading and altitude. Ensure that your airspeed is at or below maneuvering speed. (V_A)

Using a prominent landmark or section lines extending to horizon as a reference to begin the steep turn helps you determine when to begin the rollout.

② Establish the turn. Roll into a 45° angle of bank turn at or below V_A. During roll-in, smoothly add power and slowly increase back pressure on the control wheel to maintain altitude. Maintain coordinated flight and trim to relieve control pressures.

As you enter the turn, establish the bank at a moderate rate. If you roll the airplane too rapidly, you can have difficulty establishing the pitch attitude necessary to maintain altitude. Do not apply too much back pressure while initially entering the turn or you will gain altitude. However, as you become established in the turn, you will need greater back pressure to maintain altitude.

③ Maintain the angle of bank and altitude. Confirm your attitude by referring to both the natural horizon and attitude indicator. Verify the correct bank angle by referring to the attitude indicator. Use the altimeter and vertical speed indicator to determine if changes in pitch are required.

To maintain bank angle and altitude, observe the relative position of the horizon to the nose and the wings when the airplane is at the proper attitude. Maintain that site picture throughout the turn.

If you are losing altitude in the turn, decrease the angle of bank first, then increase back pressure on the control wheel to raise the nose. After you regain your desired altitude, roll back to the desired angle of bank.

④ **Roll out on the entry heading and altitude.** Lead the roll-out heading by 1/2 of the bank angle (approximately 20°). During roll-out, gradually decrease back pressure on the control wheel and reduce power to maintain altitude and airspeed. Trim to relieve control pressures.

During steep turns, you will encounter an overbanking tendency that is less apparent in right turns than it is in left turns. Torque and P-factor tend to roll the aircraft to the left and work against the overbanking tendency during a right turn. Generally, you need more rudder and aileron pressure during the roll-out than you needed during the roll-in. This is because the control pressures exerted during the roll-out must overcome the airplane's overbanking tendency.

You might be instructed to perform a turn in the opposite direction immediately after rolling out of the first turn.

V. Performance and Ground Reference Maneuvers

Task	A. Steep Turns
References	FAA-H-8083-2, FAA-H-8083-3; POH/AFM
Objective	To determine that the applicant exhibits satisfactory knowledge, risk management, and skills associated with steep turns. **Note:** See Appendix 7: Aircraft, Equipment, and Operational Requirements & Limitations.
Knowledge	The applicant demonstrates understanding of:
PA.V.A.K1	Purpose of steep turns.
PA.V.A.K2	Aerodynamics associated with steep turns, to include:
PA.V.A.K2a	a. Coordinated and uncoordinated flight
PA.V.A.K2b	b. Overbanking tendencies
PA.V.A.K2c	c. Maneuvering speed, including the impact of weight changes
PA.V.A.K2d	d. Load factor and accelerated stalls
PA.V.A.K2e	e. Rate and radius of turn
Risk Management	The applicant demonstrates the ability to identify, assess and mitigate risks, encompassing:
PA.V.A.R1	Failure to divide attention between airplane control and orientation.
PA.V.A.R2	Collision hazards, to include aircraft, terrain, obstacles, and wires.
PA.V.A.R3	Low altitude maneuvering including stall, spin, or CFIT.
PA.V.A.R4	Distractions, loss of situational awareness, and/or improper task management.
PA.V.A.R5	Failure to maintain coordinated flight.
Skills	The applicant demonstrates the ability to:
PA.V.A.S1	Clear the area.
PA.V.A.S2	Establish the manufacturer's recommended airspeed or; if one is not available, a safe airspeed not to exceed V_A.
PA.V.A.S3	Roll into a coordinated 360° steep turn with approximately a 45° bank.
PA.V.A.S4	Perform the Task in the opposite direction, as specified by evaluator.
PA.V.A.S5	Maintain the entry altitude ±100 feet, airspeed ±10 knots, bank ±5°, and roll out on the entry heading ±10°.

MANEUVER 22 ■ **Steep Turns**

MANEUVER 22 ■ **Steep Turns**

EXERCISES — FLIGHT MANEUVERS

18 — SLOW FLIGHT

1. What speed should you maintain during slow flight?

2. What is the minimum AGL altitude at which you should plan to recover from slow flight?

3. What is the first step for performing slow flight?
   A. Lower the flaps in increments and trim to relieve control pressures.
   B. Reduce power, and gradually apply back pressure on the control stick to maintain altitude.
   C. Increase power to maintain altitude and apply right rudder to counteract the left-turning tendency.

4. True/False. When you add power to maintain altitude at a slow airspeed, you will need to increase right rudder pressure.

5. When recovering from slow flight, what technique should you use to retract the flaps?

19 — POWER-OFF STALLS

1. In what airplane configuration do you normally perform power-off stalls?

2. When does a typical mechanical stall warning activate?

3. Define impending stall and full stall.

4. How do you recover from a power-off stall?

5. What bank angle should you use during a turning stall? _____

20 — POWER-ON STALLS

1. In which phase(s) of flight would a power-on stall most likely occur?

2. In what airplane configuration do you normally perform power-on stalls?

3. What is the first step to perform a power-on stall?
    A. Reduce power to idle and extend flaps in increments to establish a normal glide.
    B. Reduce power and slow the airplane to takeoff speed using back pressure on the control stick to maintain altitude.
    C. Set takeoff power (or the recommended climb power setting) and apply back pressure to maintain altitude.

4. How do you induce a power-on stall?

    _____

    _____

5. As you approach a power-on stall in a right turn, will the angle of bank tend to increase or decrease? _____

21 — DEMONSTRATED STALLS

1. True/False. An applicant for a private pilot certificate is required to demonstrate flight in cross-control stalls and spins.

2. What is a cause of a secondary stall?

    _____

3. What is an accelerated stall?

    _____

4. What is an example of a situation in the traffic pattern during which a cross-control stall could occur?

    _____

5. What is an example of an action that could lead to an elevator trim stall?

    _____

6. What is the first step for spin recovery recommended by the FAA?

    _____

22 — STEEP TURNS

1. What angle of bank is normally used for steep turns? _____

2. Is overbanking tendency more apparent in a right or left turn? _____

3. How should you correct for a loss of altitude during a steep turn?

    _____

4. How much should you lead your roll-out from a steep turn? _____

5. True/False. In comparison to the roll-in, you need more rudder and aileron pressure during the roll-out from a steep turn. _____

CHAPTER 6

Ground Reference Maneuvers

EMERGENCY LANDING SITES

Because the ground reference maneuvers you learn during your flight training are practiced at relatively low altitude, you should always be vigilant for appropriate emergency landing sites. Good choices for emergency landing sites might be open pastures, turf farms, and hard-packed dirt fields. A road is not always a good option because some might have power lines, trees, or heavy traffic.

25 — Rectangular Course

The objectives of the rectangular course are to help you develop the skill to compensate for effects of the wind and to prepare you to fly the airport traffic pattern. This maneuver requires you to combine several actions:

- Divide your attention between the flight path, ground-based references, controlling the airplane, cross checking the instruments, and scanning for hazards outside the airplane.
- Adjust the bank angle during turns to correct for groundspeed changes.
- Roll out from a turn with the proper wind correction angle (crab) to compensate for wind drift.
- Establish the proper crab angle to maintain the track over the ground during the straight flight segments.
- Maintain a constant altitude throughout the maneuver.

Clear the area for traffic and check to ensure there are no obstructions such as towers or power lines. Also, select an emergency landing area within gliding distance. You typically fly the pattern using left turns (although you should also practice right-hand patterns) and at a distance of approximately 1/4 to 1/2 mile outside the field boundary. If you fly too close to the boundaries, the bank angle in the turns will be excessive (greater than 45°) and you might have difficulty keeping the edges of the field in sight. While flying the maneuver, maintain coordinated flight and trim to relieve control pressures, as needed.

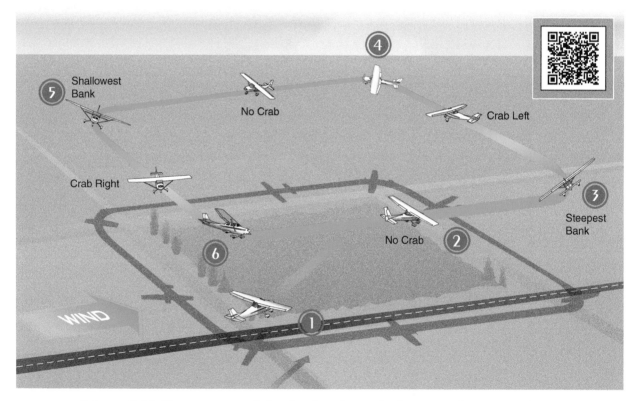

1 Select a field. Choose a rectangle bordered on four sides by section lines or roads away from a populated area. The field should have sides between 1/2 and 1 mile in length. Ensure the wind is blowing parallel to the long side of the rectangle, if possible.

To fly a precise course, ensure you accurately estimate the wind direction before starting the maneuver. Although you can use the direction of the wind at your departure airport as a guide, check for other signs of wind direction near your selected field, such as blowing trees, smoke, dust, and wave patterns on water and grain fields. You also can fly a 360° constant airspeed, constant bank angle turn and note the airplane's drift to determine the wind direction.

MANEUVER 23 ▪ **Rectangular Course**

Enter the downwind leg. Enter the maneuver at a 45° angle to the downwind leg. Use an altitude of 600 to 1,000 feet AGL, and fly parallel to the field boundary at a distance of 1/4 to 1/2 mile away.

 Turn crosswind from downwind. Use the steepest bank angle of the four turns to compensate for high groundspeed. Decrease the bank angle as your groundspeed decreases. Turn more than 90° to crab into the wind on the crosswind leg.

> The amount of bank you use is a function of groundspeed; the greater the groundspeed, the greater the angle of bank required. Limit the bank angle to under 45°.

 Turn upwind. Decrease the bank angle as the headwind increases and your groundspeed decreases. If you were holding a crab angle into the wind on the crosswind leg, turn less than 90° to fly parallel to the field boundary on the upwind leg.

> Do not focus so much on the ground references that you forget to maintain situational awareness. Ensure you are cross checking the flight instruments and scanning for traffic.

 Turn crosswind from upwind. Use the shallowest bank angle of the four turns to compensate for low groundspeed. Increase the bank angle as your groundspeed increases. Turn less than 90° to crab into the wind on the crosswind leg.

 Turn downwind. When you are abeam the downwind segment of the field boundary, begin a turn to the downwind leg. Because you were holding a crab angle to compensate for the crosswind, you will need to turn greater than 90° to parallel the downwind field boundary.

MANEUVER 23 ▪ Rectangular Course

V. Performance and Ground Reference Maneuvers

Task	B. Ground Reference Maneuvers
References	14 CFR part 61; FAA-H-8083-2, FAA-H-8083-3
Objective	To determine that the applicant exhibits satisfactory knowledge, risk management, and skills associated with ground reference maneuvering which may include a rectangular course, S-turns, and turns around a point. **Note:** See *Appendix 7: Aircraft, Equipment, and Operational Requirements & Limitations*.
Knowledge	The applicant demonstrates understanding of:
PA.V.B.K1	Purpose of ground reference maneuvers.
PA.V.B.K2	Effects of wind on ground track and relation to a ground reference point.
PA.V.B.K3	Effects of bank angle and groundspeed on rate and radius of turn.
PA.V.B.K4	Relationship of rectangular course to airport traffic pattern.
Risk Management	The applicant demonstrates the ability to identify, assess and mitigate risks, encompassing:
PA.V.B.R1	Failure to divide attention between airplane control and orientation.
PA.V.B.R2	Collision hazards, to include aircraft, terrain, obstacles, and wires.
PA.V.B.R3	Low altitude maneuvering including stall, spin, or CFIT.
PA.V.B.R4	Distractions, loss of situational awareness, and/or improper task management.
PA.V.B.R5	Failure to maintain coordinated flight.
Skills	The applicant demonstrates the ability to:
PA.V.B.S1	Clear the area.
PA.V.B.S2	Select a suitable ground reference area, line, or point as appropriate.
PA.V.B.S3	Plan the maneuver: **Note:** The evaluator must select at least one maneuver for the applicant to demonstrate.
PA.V.B.S3a	a. Rectangular course: enter a left or right pattern, 600 to 1,000 feet above ground level (AGL) at an appropriate distance from the selected reference area, 45° to the downwind leg
PA.V.B.S3b	b. S-turns: enter perpendicular to the selected reference line, 600 to 1,000 feet AGL at an appropriate distance from the selected reference area
PA.V.B.S3c	c. Turns around a point: enter at an appropriate distance from the reference point, 600 to 1,000 feet AGL at an appropriate distance from the selected reference area
PA.V.B.S4	Apply adequate wind-drift correction during straight and turning flight to maintain a constant ground track around a rectangular reference area, or to maintain a constant radius turn on each side of a selected reference line or point.
PA.V.B.S5	If performing S-Turns, reverse the turn directly over the selected reference line; if performing turns around a point, complete turns in either direction, as specified by the evaluator.
PA.V.B.S6	Divide attention between airplane control, traffic avoidance and the ground track while maintaining coordinated flight.
PA.V.B.S7	Maintain altitude ±100 feet; maintain airspeed ±10 knots.

26 — S-Turns

An S-turn is a ground reference maneuver that helps you improve your ability to compensate for wind drift during turns. The S-turn maneuver consists of a series of uniform 180° turns in opposite directions crossing and recrossing a straight road, fence line, or section line. The maneuver requires many of the same techniques used for the rectangular course, including dividing your attention between the ground reference line and airplane control and changing bank angle to compensate for the effects of the wind. Clear the area for traffic and check to ensure there are no obstructions such as towers or power lines. Select an emergency landing area within gliding distance. While flying the maneuver, maintain coordinated flight and trim to relieve control pressures, as needed.

MANEUVER 24 ▪ **S - Turns**

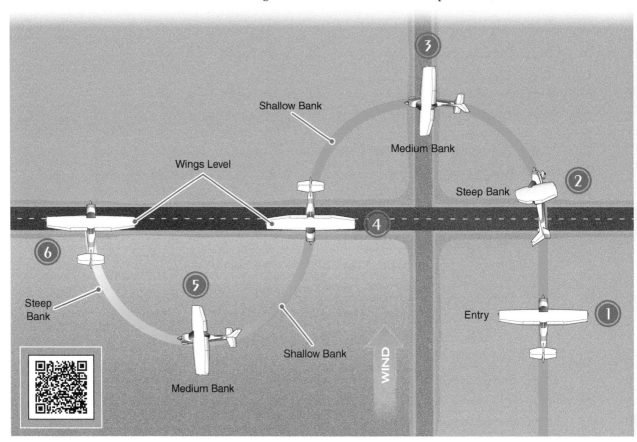

① **Select a ground reference.** Choose a road, fence line, or section line that is long enough to enable you to complete at lease two turns. Ensure the wind is blowing perpendicular to the reference line.

② **Enter downwind perpendicular to the road.** Maintain 600 to 1.000 feet AGL. As you cross the road, immediately roll into a turn. Use a relatively steep bank angle to compensate for high groundspeed.

> Pitching up and down to maintain altitude will cause your airspeed, and consequently your groundspeed, to vary. In this case, accurately assessing the effects of the wind and properly adjusting your bank angle are difficult.

③ **Track a half circle.** Use a medium bank angle and crab into the wind when flying directly crosswind. After you pass the 90° point, decrease the bank angle as the headwind increases and your groundspeed decreases.

④ **Cross the reference line upwind.** Roll out of the turn with the wings level over the road. Roll into a turn in the opposite direction. Use a relatively shallow bank angle to compensate for low groundspeed.

Increasing the bank angle too rapidly during the initial part of the turn on the upwind side will prevent completion of 180° of turn before recrossing the reference line. To avoid this error, visualize your ground track and remember that a slow groundspeed requires a shallower angle of bank and, conversely, a high groundspeed requires a steeper bank angle.

⑤ **Track another half circle.** Use a medium bank angle and crab into the wind when flying directly crosswind. After you pass the 90° point, increase the bank angle as the tailwind and your groundspeed increase.

⑥ **Cross the reference line downwind.** Roll out of the turn with the wings level over the road. Roll into a turn in the opposite direction if you are starting another turn.

The Private Pilot Airman Certification Standards (ACS) for Ground Reference Maneuvers apply to Rectangular Course, S-Turns, and Turns Around a Point. See Maneuver 25 — Rectangular Course, page 6-3.

MANEUVER 24 ▪ **S - Turns**

27 — Turns Around a Point

Like S-turns and the rectangular course, turns around a point are intended to help you develop the ability to control the airplane while compensating for wind effects and dividing your attention between the flight path and a ground reference point. During the maneuver, you are required to maintain a constant radius turn around a reference point while maintaining a constant altitude. You should plan to begin the maneuver from a downwind entry at 600 feet to 1,000 feet AGL. Initially perform the turns to the left and do not exceed a 45° angle of bank.

If any wind exists, a constantly changing angle of bank will be required to maintain a uniform radius around a point. The closer the airplane is to a direct downwind heading where the groundspeed is the greatest, the steeper the bank required. Conversely, the more nearly the airplane is to a direct upwind heading where the groundspeed is least, the shallower the bank required. As always, you should maintain coordinated flight and trim to relieve control pressures, as needed, throughout the maneuver.

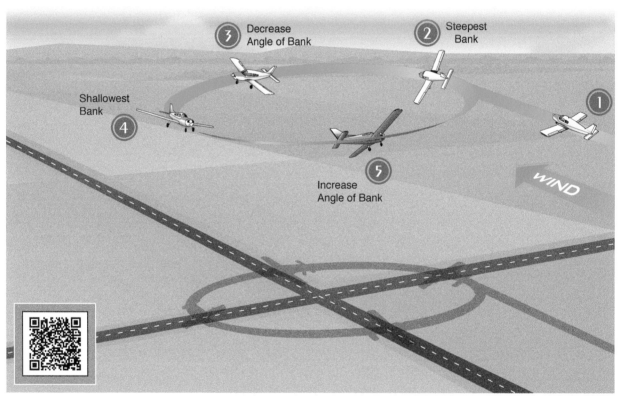

① **Select a ground reference point.** Choose a landmark that is easy to see from all directions, away from populated areas and within gliding distance of a suitable emergency landing field.

> You can use trees, isolated haystacks, or other small landmarks. An intersection of roads or fence lines is more desirable, because the wing might momentarily block your view of the reference point during the maneuver. By selecting a road or fence line intersection, you can mentally project these lines to their logical intersection and maintain your orientation.

② **Enter the turn downwind.** Maintain 600 to 1.000 feet AGL. Roll into the turn when the reference point is abeam the airplane. Use a relatively steep bank angle to compensate for high groundspeed.

> If you do not establish the proper lateral distance between your position and the reference point, the wing can block your view of the reference point.

Turn crosswind from downwind. Decrease the bank angle as the tailwind and groundspeed decrease. Use a medium bank and crab into the wind when flying directly crosswind.

Pitching up and down to maintain altitude will cause your airspeed, and consequently your groundspeed, to vary. In this case, accurately assessing the effects of the wind and properly adjusting your bank angle are difficult.

 Turn upwind. Decrease the bank angle as the headwind increases and your groundspeed decreases. Use the shallowest bank angle when flying directly upwind.

When heading directly upwind, you normally are at or near level flight.

 Complete the first turn.

- As you turn crosswind from upwind, increase the bank angle as the headwind decreases and your groundspeed increases. Use a medium bank and crab into the wind when flying directly crosswind.

- As you turn downwind from crosswind, increase the bank angle as the tailwind and groundspeed increase.

The Private Pilot Airman Certification Standards (ACS) for Ground Reference Maneuvers apply to Rectangular Course, S-Turns, and Turns Around a Point. See Maneuver 25 — Rectangular Course, page 6-3.

MANEUVER 25 ▪ **Turns Around a Point**

EXERCISES — GROUND REFERENCE MANEUVERS

25 — RECTANGULAR COURSE

1. What other maneuver with similar dimensions does the rectangular course prepare you to fly?

2. What factors should you consider when selecting an area to perform a rectangular course?

3. What is the maximum bank angle you should use when performing a rectangular course?

4. When should you begin your turn from the downwind leg to the crosswind leg?

5. Which turn should have the shallowest angle of bank when flying a rectangular course?

26 — S-TURNS

1. During S-turns, how should the ground reference line be oriented with regard to the wind direction?

2. True/False. To begin an S-turn, you should roll into a relatively shallow bank as you cross the ground reference line.

3. When you turn from a downwind heading to an upwind heading, how will your groundspeed change?

4. Why should you change your angle of bank when turning from a tailwind to a headwind?

5. When should the airplane's wings be level during an S-turn?

EXERCISES ▪ **Ground Reference Maneuvers**

27 — TURNS AROUND A POINT

1. Why is the intersection of roads or fence lines a desirable reference point?

_____

2. Relative to the wind direction, which direction should you enter a turn around a point?

_____

3. What is the maximum angle of bank normally used when flying turns around a point?

_____

4. When flying turns around a point, where does the steepest bank angle occur?

_____

5. When flying turns around a point, where does the shallowest bank angle occur?

_____

EXERCISES ■ **Ground Reference Maneuvers**

CHAPTER 7

Performance Takeoffs and Landings

28 — Short-Field Takeoff and Maximum Performance Climb

Short-field takeoff and maximum performance climb procedures are required when the usable runway length is short, or when the runway available for takeoff is restricted by obstructions, such as trees, powerlines, or buildings, at the departure end. During short-field practice sessions, assume that you are departing from a short runway and that you must clear an obstacle which is 50 feet in height. To accomplish successful short-field takeoffs and climbs you must be familiar with the best angle-of-climb speed (V_X) and the best rate-of-climb speed (V_Y) for your airplane. Many manufacturers also specify a best obstacle clearance speed. Consult your airplane's AFM/POH for the appropriate speeds and specific procedures for performing short-field takeoffs. Because the same general procedures to perform a normal takeoff and climb apply, the following step-by-step procedure only emphasizes procedures specific to short-field takeoffs and climbs.

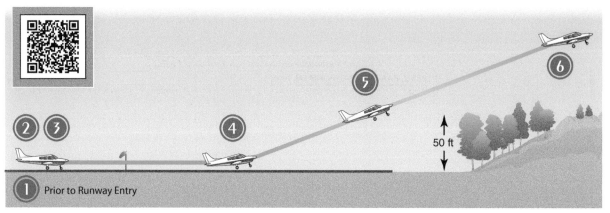

1. Prior to Runway Entry

① **Prepare for takeoff.** Complete the before takeoff check. Include a review of the short-field procedure in your takeoff briefing. Set the flaps as recommended in the AFM/POH.

> The appropriate flap setting varies between airplanes and can range from no flaps to approximately 1/2 flaps.

② **Taxi onto the runway.** Taxi into position at the beginning of the runway to maximize the use of available runway. Line up with the centerline and ensure the nosewheel is straight before applying the brakes.

> Prior to taxiing onto the runway, remember to clear the runway and approach and departure paths, and obtain a clearance (at a controlled airport) or self announce your intentions (at an uncontrolled airport).

③ **Add takeoff power.** Hold the brakes until the airplane achieves full power. Check the engine indications to verify that the engine is developing full power and operating within its limits and then release the brakes.

> Holding the brakes until you achieve full power enables you to determine that the engine is functioning properly before you take off from a field where power availability is critical and the distance to reject a takeoff is limited.

④ **Accelerate to liftoff.** Accelerate with the airplane's full weight on the main wheels by holding neutral elevator/stabilator. Add back pressure on the control wheel to lift off at the recommended airspeed.

> Avoid raising the nose prior to the recommended liftoff speed. A premature nose-high attitude produces drag and a longer takeoff roll. If you attempt to lift the airplane off the runway prematurely, or to climb too steeply, the airplane can settle back to the runway, stall, or impact the obstacle.

Establish the initial climb. Establish a pitch attitude to maintain the best angle of climb speed (V_X) or obstacle clearance speed recommended in the AFM/POH. Maintain this speed until you clear the obstacle or until the airplane is 50 feet above the surface.

> Because the airplane can accelerate quickly after liftoff, you might need to apply additional back pressure to establish and maintain V_X or best obstacle clearance speed.

 Stabilize the climb. Lower the nose and accelerate to V_Y after the airplane has cleared the obstacle and reached a safe altitude, Retract the landing gear (if applicable) and then retract the flaps (if applicable). Trim to relieve control pressures and complete the Climb checklist.

> Until the airplane has cleared all obstacles, focus outside the airplane instead of looking inside the airplane or reaching for the landing gear or flap controls.

IV. Takeoffs, Landings, and Go-Arounds

Task	E. Short-Field Takeoff and Maximum Performance Climb (ASEL, AMEL)
References	FAA-H-8083-2, FAA-H-8083-3; POH/AFM; AIM
Objective	To determine that the applicant exhibits satisfactory knowledge, risk management, and skills associated with a short-field takeoff, maximum performance climb operations, and rejected takeoff procedures.
Knowledge	The applicant demonstrates understanding of:
PA.IV.E.K1	Effects of atmospheric conditions, including wind, on takeoff and climb performance.
PA.IV.E.K2	V_X and V_Y.
PA.IV.E.K3	Appropriate airplane configuration.
Risk Management	The applicant demonstrates the ability to identify, assess and mitigate risks, encompassing:
PA.IV.E.R1	Selection of runway based on pilot capability, airplane performance and limitations, available distance, and wind.
PA.IV.E.R2	Effects of:
PA.IV.E.R2a	a. Crosswind
PA.IV.E.R2b	b. Windshear
PA.IV.E.R2c	c. Tailwind
PA.IV.E.R2d	d. Wake turbulence
PA.IV.E.R2e	e. Runway surface/condition
PA.IV.E.R3	Abnormal operations, to include planning for:
PA.IV.E.R3a	a. Rejected takeoff
PA.IV.E.R3b	b. Engine failure in takeoff/climb phase of flight
PA.IV.E.R4	Collision hazards, to include aircraft, vehicles, persons, wildlife, terrain, obstacles, and wires.
PA.IV.E.R5	Low altitude maneuvering including stall, spin, or CFIT.
PA.IV.E.R6	Distractions, loss of situational awareness, and/or improper task management.
Skills	The applicant demonstrates the ability to:
PA.IV.E.S1	Complete the appropriate checklist.
PA.IV.E.S2	Make radio calls as appropriate.
PA.IV.E.S3	Verify assigned/correct runway.
PA.IV.E.S4	Ascertain wind direction with or without visible wind direction indicators.
PA.IV.E.S5	Position the flight controls for the existing wind conditions.
PA.IV.E.S6	Clear the area, taxi into takeoff position and align the airplane on the runway centerline utilizing maximum available takeoff area.
PA.IV.E.S7	Apply brakes while setting engine power to achieve maximum performance.
PA.IV.E.S8	Confirm takeoff power prior to brake release and verify proper engine and flight instrument indications prior to rotation.
PA.IV.E.S9	Rotate and lift off at the recommended airspeed and accelerate to the recommended obstacle clearance airspeed or V_X, +10/-5 knots.
PA.IV.E.S10	Establish a pitch attitude that will maintain the recommended obstacle clearance airspeed or V_X, +10/-5 knots until the obstacle is cleared or until the airplane is 50 feet above the surface.
PA.IV.E.S11	After clearing the obstacle, establish pitch attitude for V_Y and accelerate to and maintain V_Y +10/-5 knots during the climb.
PA.IV.E.S12	Configure the airplane in accordance with the manufacturer's guidance after a positive rate of climb has been verified.
PA.IV.E.S13	Maintain V_Y +10/-5 knots to a safe maneuvering altitude.
PA.IV.E.S14	Maintain directional control and proper wind-drift correction throughout takeoff and climb.
PA.IV.E.S15	Comply with noise abatement procedures.

MANEUVER 28 ▪ **Short-Field Takeoff and Climb**

29 — Short-Field Approach and Landing

A short-field landing is necessary when you have a relatively short landing area or when an approach must be made over obstacles that limit the available landing area. A short-field landing consists of a steep approach over an obstacle, using power and flaps (normally full flaps). A minimum landing speed is desired with a touchdown point as close to the threshold as possible. During short-field landing practice, assume you are making the approach and landing over a 50-foot obstacle. You should consult your airplane's AFM/POH for the appropriate speeds and specific procedures for performing short-field landings. Because the same general procedures to perform a normal approach and landing apply, the following step-by-step procedure only emphasizes procedures specific to short-field approaches and landings.

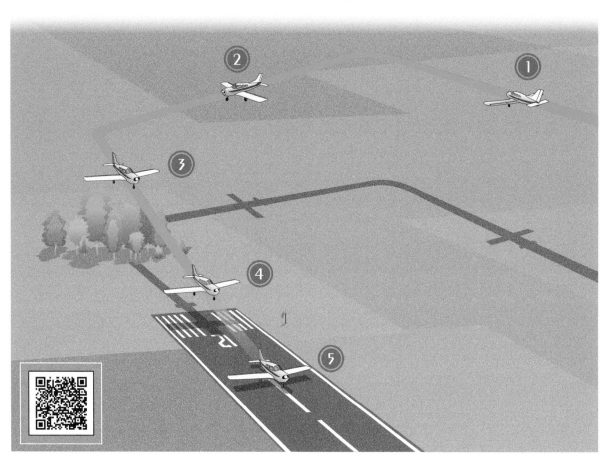

1. **Prepare for landing.** Ensure that you have reviewed and briefed the short-field landing procedure. Clear the area for traffic. Follow the Before Landing checklist to complete each item at the appropriate time, including extending flaps.

2. **Stabilize the approach.** Assess your situation at the key position. Make any needed adjustments to altitude, airspeed, and distance from the runway to ensure obstacle clearance on final. Extend flaps as appropriate based on your assessment.

> You typically extend approximately 1/3 of the available flaps during the latter portion of the downwind leg and 2/3 on base, while progressively reducing the airspeed.

Turn final. Begin the final approach at least 500 feet higher than the touchdown area. Extend the remaining flaps as appropriate. Maintain the short-field approach speed recommended in the AFM/POH.

> The descent angle for the short-field approach is steeper than that for a normal approach to allow the airplane to clear an obstacle located near the approach end of the runway. Extending full flaps allows a steeper descent angle without an increase in airspeed, which results in a decrease in the distance required to bring the airplane to a full stop.

 Flare and touch down. Reduce the power smoothly to idle, Allow the airplane to settle to the runway on the main landing gear in a nose-high attitude as it approaches stall speed. As you begin the flare, reduce power smoothly to idle and allow the airplane to touch down in a full-stall condition. Touch down within 200 feet of a specified point with minimum float.

> Because the short-field approach is made at a steep descent angle and close to the airplane's stalling speed, you must accurately judge when to initiate the flare to avoid flying into the ground or stalling prematurely and sinking rapidly
>
> Reducing power too rapidly can cause an immediate increase in the rate of descent and a hard landing. On the other hand, the airplane should touch down with little or no float. An excessive amount of airspeed can cause the airplane to touch down too far beyond the runway threshold and exceed the available landing area during roll-out.

 Roll out. Lower the nose when the airplane is firmly on the runway. Retract the flaps as recommended by the AFM/POH. Apply the brakes as necessary to safely stop in the shortest distance.

> Some manufacturers recommend retraction of flaps on the landing roll, which transfers more weight to the main gear to enhance braking.

MANEUVER 29 ■ **Short-Field Approach and Landing**

IV. Takeoffs, Landings, and Go-Arounds

Task	F. Short-Field Approach and Landing (ASEL, AMEL)
References	FAA-H-8083-2, FAA-H-8083-3; POH/AFM; AIM
Objective	To determine that the applicant exhibits satisfactory knowledge, risk management, and skills associated with a short-field approach and landing with emphasis on proper use and coordination of flight controls.
Knowledge	The applicant demonstrates understanding of:
PA.IV.F.K1	A stabilized approach, to include energy management concepts.
PA.IV.F.K2	Effects of atmospheric conditions, including wind, on approach and landing performance.
PA.IV.F.K3	Wind correction techniques on approach and landing.
Risk Management	The applicant demonstrates the ability to identify, assess and mitigate risks, encompassing:
PA.IV.F.R1	Selection of runway based on pilot capability, airplane performance and limitations, available distance, and wind.
PA.IV.F.R2	Effects of:
PA.IV.F.R2a	a. Crosswind
PA.IV.F.R2b	b. Windshear
PA.IV.F.R2c	c. Tailwind
PA.IV.F.R2d	d. Wake turbulence
PA.IV.F.R2e	e. Runway surface/condition
PA.IV.F.R3	Planning for:
PA.IV.F.R3a	a. Go-around and rejected landing
PA.IV.F.R3b	b. Land and hold short operations (LAHSO)
PA.IV.F.R4	Collision hazards, to include aircraft, vehicles, persons, wildlife, terrain, obstacles, and wires.
PA.IV.F.R5	Low altitude maneuvering including stall, spin, or CFIT.
PA.IV.F.R6	Distractions, loss of situational awareness, and/or improper task management.
Skills	The applicant demonstrates the ability to:
PA.IV.F.S1	Complete the appropriate checklist.
PA.IV.F.S2	Make radio calls as appropriate.
PA.IV.F.S3	Ensure the airplane is aligned with the correct/assigned runway.
PA.IV.F.S4	Scan the landing runway and adjoining area for traffic and obstructions.
PA.IV.F.S5	Consider the wind conditions, landing surface, obstructions, and select a suitable touchdown point.
PA.IV.F.S6	Establish the recommended approach and landing configuration and airspeed, and adjust pitch attitude and power as required to maintain a stabilized approach.
PA.IV.F.S7	Maintain manufacturer's published airspeed or in its absence not more than 1.3 V_{SO}, +10/-5 knots with gust factor applied.
PA.IV.F.S8	Maintain crosswind correction and directional control throughout the approach and landing.
PA.IV.F.S9	Make smooth, timely, and correct control application during the round out and touchdown.
PA.IV.F.S10	Touch down at a proper pitch attitude, within 200 feet beyond or on the specified point, threshold markings or runway numbers, with no side drift, minimum float, and with the airplane's longitudinal axis aligned with and over runway centerline.
PA.IV.F.S11	Use manufacturer's recommended procedures for airplane configuration and braking.
PA.IV.F.S12	Execute a timely go-around if the approach cannot be made within the tolerances specified above or for any other condition that may result in an unsafe approach or landing.
PA.IV.F.S13	Utilize runway incursion avoidance procedures.

MANEUVER 29 ■ **Short-Field Approach and Landing**

30 — Soft-Field Takeoff and Climb

Applying normal takeoff techniques when taking off from a soft surface reduces the airplane's ability to accelerate during the takeoff roll and can prevent the airplane from reaching adequate takeoff speed The objective of the soft-field takeoff is to transfer the weight of the airplane from the landing gear to the wings as quickly and smoothly as possible to eliminate the drag caused by surfaces such as tall grass, soft dirt, or snow. The soft-field technique allows the airplane to be airborne as quickly as possible and can also be useful on a rough field to avoid damaging the landing gear.

Takeoffs and climbs from soft fields require knowledge of your airplane's performance characteristics, such as how to determine takeoff distance for soft fields, the proper use of V_X and V_Y, and how ground effect applies to takeoffs. Because the same general procedures to perform a normal takeoff and climb apply, the following step-by-step procedure only emphasizes procedures specific to soft-field takeoffs.

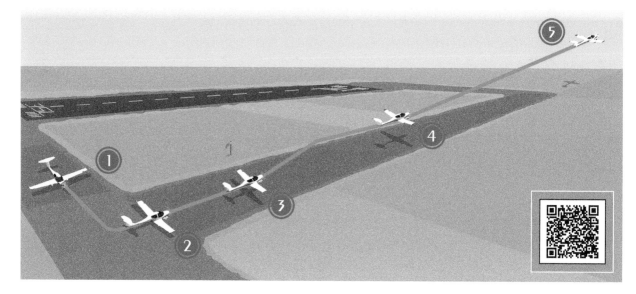

① **Prepare for takeoff.** To avoid propeller damage and the possibility of the airplane becoming stuck, complete the Before Takeoff checklist on a paved or firm surface area, if practical. Review the soft-field takeoff procedure during the takeoff briefing and set the flaps as recommended by the AFM/POH.

② **Taxi onto the runway and begin the takeoff.** Apply full back pressure on the control stick to reduce weight on the nosewheel while taxiing. Line up with the center of the runway and while still rolling, apply takeoff power. Initially, continue to maintain full back pressure on the control stick.

> Prior to taxiing onto the runway, remember to clear the runway and approach and departure paths, and obtain a clearance (at a controlled airport) or self announce your intentions (at an uncontrolled airport).

③ **Accelerate to liftoff.** As the airplane accelerates, reduce back pressure slightly on the control stick to prevent the tail from hitting the runway, As the airplane lifts off, lower the nose to fly just above the surface in ground effect.

> If you do not release some back pressure while accelerating during the takeoff roll, the airplane can assume an extremely nose-high attitude, which can cause the tail skid to come in contact with the runway.
>
> As the airspeed increases, lift increases and more of the aircraft's weight is transferred to the wings causing the airplane to become airborne at an airspeed slower than safe climb speed so you must accelerate in ground effect.

On a rough surface the airplane can skip or bounce into the air before its full weight can be supported aerodynamically. Therefore, hold the pitch attitude as constant as possible (an important application of slow flight). If you permit the nose to lower after a bounce, the nosewheel can strike the ground. On the other hand, sharply increasing the pitch attitude after a bounce can cause the airplane to stall.

 Establish the initial climb. Allow the airplane to accelerate in ground effect to V_X or V_Y (as appropriate). Pitch up to maintain V_X or V_Y and begin the climb.

Attempting to climb prematurely or too steeply can cause the airplane to settle back to the surface as a result of the loss of ground effect. During the transition out of ground effect, do not try to climb before reaching V_X or V_Y. To establish the correct pitch attitude during this transition you must have a good understanding of the control pressures, aircraft responses, visual clues, and acceleration characteristics of your specific airplane

Stabilize the climb. Lower the nose and accelerate to V_Y after the airplane has cleared any obstacles and reached a safe altitude, Retract the landing gear (if applicable) and then retract the flaps (if applicable). Trim to relieve control pressures and complete the Climb checklist.

IV. Takeoffs, Landings, and Go-Arounds

Task	C. Soft-Field Takeoff and Climb (ASEL)
References	FAA-H-8083-2, FAA-H-8083-3; POH/AFM; AIM
Objective	To determine that the applicant exhibits satisfactory knowledge, risk management, and skills associated with a soft-field takeoff, climb operations, and rejected takeoff procedures.
Knowledge	The applicant demonstrates understanding of:
PA.IV.C.K1	Effects of atmospheric conditions, including wind, on takeoff and climb performance.
PA.IV.C.K2	V_X and V_Y.
PA.IV.C.K3	Appropriate airplane configuration.
PA.IV.C.K4	Ground effect.
PA.IV.C.K5	Importance of weight transfer from wheels to wings.
PA.IV.C.K6	Left turning tendencies.
Risk Management	The applicant demonstrates the ability to identify, assess and mitigate risks, encompassing:
PA.IV.C.R1	Selection of runway based on pilot capability, airplane performance and limitations, available distance, and wind.
PA.IV.C.R2	Effects of:
PA.IV.C.R2a	a. Crosswind
PA.IV.C.R2b	b. Windshear
PA.IV.C.R2c	c. Tailwind
PA.IV.C.R2d	d. Wake turbulence
PA.IV.C.R2e	e. Runway surface/condition
PA.IV.C.R3	Abnormal operations, to include planning for:
PA.IV.C.R3a	a. Rejected takeoff
PA.IV.C.R3b	b. Engine failure in takeoff/climb phase of flight
PA.IV.C.R4	Collision hazards, to include aircraft, vehicles, persons, wildlife, terrain, obstacles, and wires.
PA.IV.C.R5	Low altitude maneuvering including stall, spin, or CFIT.
PA.IV.C.R6	Distractions, loss of situational awareness, and/or improper task management.
Skills	The applicant demonstrates the ability to:
PA.IV.C.S1	Complete the appropriate checklist.
PA.IV.C.S2	Make radio calls as appropriate.
PA.IV.C.S3	Verify assigned/correct runway.
PA.IV.C.S4	Ascertain wind direction with or without visible wind direction indicators.
PA.IV.C.S5	Position the flight controls for the existing wind conditions.
PA.IV.C.S6	Clear the area, maintain necessary flight control inputs, taxi into takeoff position and align the airplane on the runway centerline without stopping, while advancing the throttle smoothly to takeoff power.
PA.IV.C.S7	Confirm takeoff power and proper engine and flight instrument indications.
PA.IV.C.S8	Establish and maintain a pitch attitude that will transfer the weight of the airplane from the wheels to the wings as rapidly as possible.
PA.IV.C.S9	Lift off at the lowest possible airspeed and remain in ground effect while accelerating to V_X or V_Y, as appropriate.
PA.IV.C.S10	Establish a pitch attitude for V_X or V_Y, as appropriate, and maintain selected airspeed +10/-5 knots during the climb.
PA.IV.C.S11	Configure the airplane after a positive rate of climb has been verified or in accordance with airplane manufacturer's instructions.
PA.IV.C.S12	Maintain V_X or V_Y, as appropriate, +10/-5 knots to a safe maneuvering altitude.
PA.IV.C.S13	Maintain directional control and proper wind-drift correction throughout takeoff and climb.
PA.IV.C.S14	Comply with noise abatement procedures.

MANEUVER 30 ■ **Soft-Field Takeoff and Climb**

31 — Soft-Field Approach and Landing

The objective of a soft-field landing is to ease the weight of the airplane from the wings to the main landing gear as gently and slowly as possible while keeping the nosewheel off the soft surface during most of the landing roll. This technique prevents the nosewheel from sinking into the soft surface (snow, dirt, tall grass etc.), minimizes stresses imposed on the landing gear by the rough/soft surface, and reduces the possibility of an abrupt stop during the landing roll. You should consult your airplane's AFM/POH for the appropriate speeds and specific procedures for performing soft-field landings. Because the same general procedures to perform a normal approach and landing apply, the following step-by-step procedure only emphasizes procedures specific to soft-field landings.

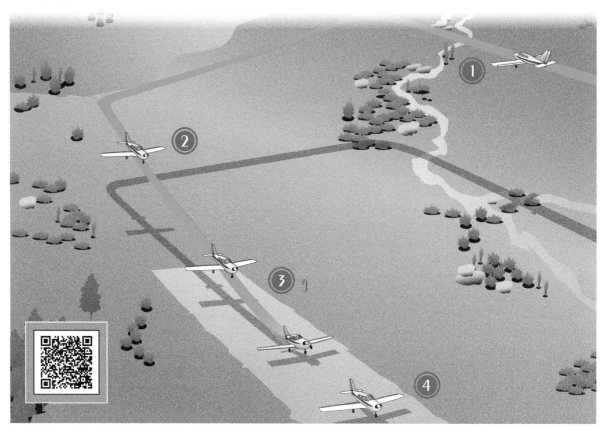

① Prepare for landing. Ensure that you have reviewed and briefed the soft-field landing procedure. Clear the area for traffic. Follow the Before Landing checklist to complete each item at the appropriate time, including extending flaps.

> You typically extend approximately 1/3 of the available flaps during the latter portion of the downwind leg and 2/3 on base, while progressively reducing the airspeed.

② Fly a stabilized final approach. Maintain the same glide path as during a normal approach unless obstacles are in the approach path. Extend the remaining flaps as appropriate. Maintain the approach speed recommended in the AFM/POH.

> The use of flaps during a soft-field landing is normally recommended to allow the airplane to touch down at a minimum speed. However, you must also consider the runway conditions when determining whether to use full flaps. For example, in a low-wing aircraft, the flaps can suffer damage from mud, slush, or stones thrown up from the wheels.

③ Flare and touch down. Hold the airplane one to two feet above the surface as long as possible to dissipate forward speed. Use power to maintain a nose-high attitude and touch down at the lowest speed possible.

When you maintain power during the landing flare and touchdown, the slipstream flow over the empennage increases the effectiveness of the elevator/stabilator. The amount of power required during the landing flare and touchdown varies with the weight and density altitude.

 Roll out. After touchdown, maintain back pressure on the control wheel to hold the nosewheel off the surface as long as practical. As the airspeed decreases, smoothly and gently lower the nosewheel to the surface. Increase the power slightly, if necessary, to keep the aircraft moving and prevent it from stopping suddenly on the soft surface. Avoid using the brakes.

Adding a small amount of power after touchdown will help you to ease the nosewheel down, under control.

Braking can cause the nosewheel to dig into the soft surface and can damage the landing gear. The soft surface should provide sufficient braking action to slow the airplane.

IV. Takeoffs, Landings, and Go-Arounds

Task	**D. Soft-Field Approach and Landing (ASEL)**
References	FAA-H-8083-2, FAA-H-8083-3; POH/AFM; AIM
Objective	To determine that the applicant exhibits satisfactory knowledge, risk management, and skills associated with a soft-field approach and landing with emphasis on proper use and coordination of flight controls.
Knowledge	The applicant demonstrates understanding of:
PA.IV.D.K1	A stabilized approach, to include energy management concepts.
PA.IV.D.K2	Effects of atmospheric conditions, including wind, on approach and landing performance.
PA.IV.D.K3	Wind correction techniques on approach and landing.
Risk Management	The applicant demonstrates the ability to identify, assess and mitigate risks, encompassing:
PA.IV.D.R1	Selection of runway based on pilot capability, airplane performance and limitations, available distance, and wind.
PA.IV.D.R2	Effects of:
PA.IV.D.R2a	a. Crosswind
PA.IV.D.R2b	b. Windshear
PA.IV.D.R2c	c. Tailwind
PA.IV.D.R2d	d. Wake turbulence
PA.IV.D.R2e	e. Runway surface/condition
PA.IV.D.R3	Planning for:
PA.IV.D.R3a	a. Go-around and rejected landing
PA.IV.D.R3b	b. Land and hold short operations (LAHSO)
PA.IV.D.R4	Collision hazards, to include aircraft, vehicles, persons, wildlife, terrain, obstacles, and wires.
PA.IV.D.R5	Low altitude maneuvering including stall, spin, or CFIT.
PA.IV.D.R6	Distractions, loss of situational awareness, and/or improper task management.
Skills	The applicant demonstrates the ability to:
PA.IV.D.S1	Complete the appropriate checklist.
PA.IV.D.S2	Make radio calls as appropriate.
PA.IV.D.S3	Ensure the airplane is aligned with the correct/assigned runway.
PA.IV.D.S4	Scan the landing runway and adjoining area for traffic and obstructions.
PA.IV.D.S5	Consider the wind conditions, landing surface, obstructions, and select a suitable touchdown point.
PA.IV.D.S6	Establish the recommended approach and landing configuration and airspeed, and adjust pitch attitude and power as required to maintain a stabilized approach.
PA.IV.D.S7	Maintain manufacturer's published airspeed or in its absence not more than $1.3\ V_{SO}$, +10/-5 knots with gust factor applied.
PA.IV.D.S8	Maintain crosswind correction and directional control throughout the approach and landing.
PA.IV.D.S9	Make smooth, timely, and correct control inputs during the round out and touchdown, and, for tricycle gear airplanes, keep the nose wheel off the surface until loss of elevator effectiveness.
PA.IV.D.S10	Touch down at a proper pitch attitude with minimum sink rate, no side drift, and with the airplane's longitudinal axis aligned with the center of the runway.
PA.IV.D.S11	Maintain elevator as recommended by manufacturer during rollout and exit the "soft" area at a speed that would preclude sinking into the surface.
PA.IV.D.S12	Execute a timely go-around if the approach cannot be made within the tolerances specified above or for any other condition that may result in an unsafe approach or landing.
PA.IV.D.S13	Maintain proper position of the flight controls and sufficient speed to taxi while on the soft surface.

MANEUVER 31 ■ **Soft-Field Approach and Landing**

MANEUVER 31 ▪ **Soft-Field Approach and Landing**

EXERCISES — PERFORMANCE TAKEOFFS AND LANDINGS

28 — SHORT-FIELD TAKEOFF AND MAXIMUM PERFORMANCE CLIMB

1. Name two situations which require the use of a short-field takeoff and climb.

2. During short-field practice sessions, it is assumed that you must clear an obstacle which is how many feet in height? _____

3. True/False. You should use the best rate-of-climb speed to clear obstacles at the departure end of the runway.

4. Why should you hold the brakes until the airplane achieves full power prior to beginning the takeoff roll?

5. Why should you avoid raising the nose prior to the recommended liftoff speed?

29 — SHORT-FIELD APPROACH AND LANDING

1. In what situations would performing a short-field approach and landing be necessary?

2. Is the descent angle for a short-field approach steeper, shallower, or the same as that flown for a normal approach to a landing? _____

3. What is the purpose of extending full flaps when performing a short-field approach?

4. True/False. When performing a short-field landing, you should reduce power to idle in the flare and allow the airplane to touch down in a full-stall condition.

5. What can occur if you maintain an excessive amount of airspeed during the short-field approach and landing?

30 — SOFT-FIELD TAKEOFF AND CLIMB

1. What is the objective of a soft-field takeoff?

2. What action should you take on a soft surface while taxing onto the runway?

3. True/False. You should hold the brakes until the airplane achieves full power prior to beginning the takeoff roll.

4. What can occur if you do not release some back pressure while accelerating during the takeoff roll?

5. What action should you take after liftoff before starting a climb?

31 — SOFT-FIELD APPROACH AND LANDING

1. What is the objective of a soft-field landing?

2. Why is extending flaps normally recommended for a soft-field approach and landing?

3. When performing a soft-field landing, why should you hold the airplane one to two feet above the runway as long as possible?

4. True/False. During a soft-field landing, you should lower the nosewheel to the surface as quickly as possible after touchdown.

5. What is the correct procedure for the roll-out after a soft-field landing?
   A. Maintain power at idle and apply heavy braking.
   B. Hold forward pressure on the control wheel/stick and avoid braking.
   C. Maintain back pressure on the control wheel/stick and increase power slightly, if necessary.

CHAPTER 8

Special Flight Operations

32 — Basic Instrument Maneuvers

The basic instrument instruction that you receive during private pilot training is not intended to prepare you for unrestricted flight into instrument meteorological conditions (IMC). Rather, the goals of this training are to develop more precise flying skills and to prepare you for an inadvertent entry into IMC. The procedure for inadvertent entry into IMC in many AFM/POHs is to perform a 180° turn to exit the conditions. Learning attitude instrument flying also provides a foundation for further training that could lead to the addition of an instrument rating. For more details on attitude instrument flying, refer to the Jeppesen *Instrument/Commercial* textbook.

ATTITUDE INSTRUMENT FLYING

Attitude instrument flying is a fundamental method for controlling an airplane by reference to instruments. Accident statistics show that pilots who have not been trained in attitude instrument flying lose control of the airplane in about 10 minutes if they are forced to rely solely on instrument reference. To successfully survive entry into IMC, you must first recognize and accept the seriousness of the situation and the need for immediate remedial action. Next maintain control of the airplane and finally, obtain the appropriate assistance from ATC to ensure a safe landing. Do not hesitate to seek help or to declare an emergency in a deteriorating situation.

After you recognize and accept the situation, you must realize that the only way to control the airplane safely is to use and trust the flight instruments. You can become disorientated and lose control if you attempt to control the airplane partially by reference to flight instruments while searching outside to confirm instrument indications.

INSTRUMENT SCAN

To effectively fly by instrument reference, you should understand each instrument's operating principles and limitations. Refer to Jeppesen's *Private Pilot* textbook for detailed descriptions of analog and primary flight display (PFD) instrument functions. When you fly solely by reference to instruments, you use an instrument scan—a methodical cross-check of the flight instruments. The radial cross-check is a scan pattern during which you spend 80 to 90 percent of flight time looking at the attitude indicator and taking only quick glances at the other flight instruments.

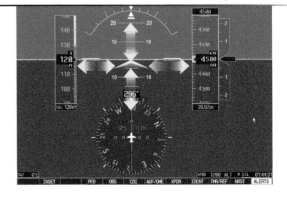

Radial Cross-Check on the PFD
The extended artificial horizon line enables you to keep the pitch attitude in your peripheral vision at all times and reduces the tendency to fixate on a specific instrument. Return your attention back to the center of the attitude indicator before proceeding to the next instrument and be sure to include the slip/skid indicator.

Performing the Radial Cross-Check
Your eyes never travel directly between the flight instruments but move by way of the attitude indicator. The maneuver being performed determines which instruments to look at in the pattern.

To enhance your ability to maintain and change attitudes when practicing attitude instrument flying, use a four-step process:

1. Establish the attitude. Use the attitude indicator as the primary reference when changing pitch or bank.

2. Trim to relieve control pressures. Use the trim to eliminate the need to apply force to the control stick to maintain the established attitude.

3. Cross check to verify the attitude. Scan and interpret the instruments to determine the magnitude of any deviations.

4. Adjust for deviations. Make small corrections for minor changes in pitch and bank using the attitude indicator as the primary reference.

TRIM

Maintain a light touch on the controls, and keep the airplane properly trimmed. If you are constantly holding control pressure, you cannot apply the precise pressures needed for controlled changes in attitude. An improperly trimmed airplane increases tension, interrupts your cross-check, and can result in abrupt or erratic control. To properly trim the airplane:

- Do not use the trim alone to establish a change in airplane attitude. Apply control pressure(s) to establish a desired attitude. Then, adjust the trim so that the aircraft maintains that attitude when you release the flight controls.

- If applicable, adjust the aileron trim to maintain a wings-level attitude and use the rudder trim to maintain coordinated flight by referring to the inclinometer or slip/skid indicator.

- Be prepared to adjust the trim anytime you change the airplane attitude, power setting, or configuration.

COMMON ERRORS

To become proficient in performing basic maneuvers by instrument reference, you should avoid three common errors associated with attitude instrument flying, fixation, omission, and emphasis.

Fixation is applying your full concentration on a single instrument and excluding all others. You might have reason to do so, such as when you suspect an instrument is malfunctioning. However, fixation typically causes errors. For example, you notice that you are 200 feet below your assigned altitude. While you fixate on the altimeter as you try to correct your altitude, you drift off of your assigned heading.

Omission is excluding one or more pertinent instruments from your scan. For example, while leveling off from a climb or descent, you might concentrate on pitch control and forget about heading or roll information.

Emphasis is relying on an instrument that you readily understand, even when it provides inadequate information, instead of relying on a combination of instruments. Although you still maintain some scan, control is degraded because you are inappropriately relying on one instrument. For example, you might be able to generally maintain altitude using the attitude indicator, but you cannot hold a precise altitude without including the altimeter in your scan.

MANEUVER 32 ■ **Basic Instrument Maneuvers**

PERFORMING INSTRUMENT MANEUVERS

When flying with a view limiting device such as JeppShades, your flight instructor will act as the safety pilot; never practice attitude instrument flight solo. The steps to perform the instrument maneuvers required for private pilot training—straight-and-level flight, constant airspeed climbs and descents, turns to headings, and recovery from unusual flight attitudes—are discussed here using a combination of analog instruments and a primary flight display (PFD). For each of these maneuvers, remember to trim to relieve control pressures each time you establish a new attitude.

STRAIGHT-AND-LEVEL FLIGHT

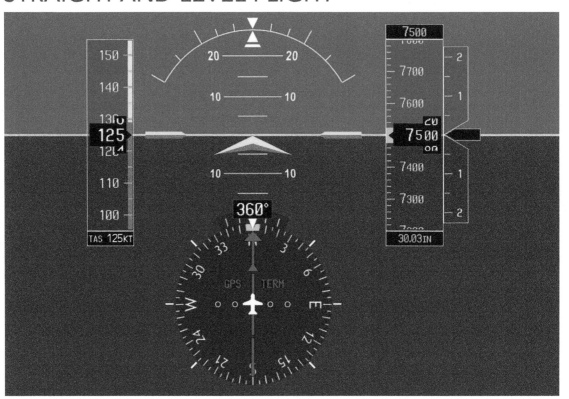

1. Position the aircraft symbol on the horizon line of the attitude indicator.

> Maintain a light touch on the controls and trim to relieve any control pressures after the airplane has stabilized in a particular attitude.

2. Use the attitude indicator as your primary reference for pitch and bank changes and cross check the other instruments.

3. Adjust the pitch when you notice changes on the:
   - Attitude indicator.
   - Altimeter. If the deviation from the desired altitude is less than 100 feet, return to the correct altitude without changing the power setting. However, if the deviation is greater than 100 feet, adjust the power and then trim to relieve control pressures.

> The trend vector on a digital altimeter shows the altitude the airplane will reach in six seconds if it continues to descend or climb at the same rate.

   - Vertical speed indicator (VSI). Use the VSI as a trend instrument for maintaining a desired pitch attitude.

> An analog VSI lags approximately six to nine seconds before displaying the correct rate of change.

MANEUVER 32 ■ Basic Instrument Maneuvers

- Airspeed indicator. The airspeed indicator indicates pitch attitude with a constant power setting—a decrease in airspeed indicates an increase in pitch attitude and vice versa. A rapid change in airspeed indicates that a large pitch change has occurred.

4. Adjust the bank when you notice changes on the:

- Attitude indicator.
- Heading indicator.

> To change heading, use a bank angle equal to 1/2 of the difference between the present heading and the desired heading (not to exceed a standard-rate turn). For example, if your desired heading is 300° and your present heading is 290°, use a bank angle no greater than 5° to change your heading by 10°.

CONSTANT AIRSPEED CLIMBS

1. Establish the climb attitude.

- Simultaneously add power and position the aircraft symbol to the desired pitch above the horizon line on the attitude indicator.
- Use the airspeed indicator and vertical speed indicator to establish the desired airspeed and rate of climb.
- Refer to the attitude indicator and heading indicator to maintain directional control.

> Remember to apply right rudder pressure as necessary to counteract the effect of P-factor.

2. Maintain the climb attitude.

- Adjust the pitch when you notice changes on the:
  - Attitude indicator.
  - Airspeed indicator.
  - Vertical speed indicator.
- Adjust the bank when you notice changes on the:
  - Attitude indicator.
  - Heading indicator.
- Cross check the altimeter to determine your progress toward the desired altitude.

3. Level off at the appropriate point.

- Refer to the altimeter to begin leveling off at approximately 10 percent of your climb rate below the desired altitude.
- Adjust the pitch to place the aircraft symbol on the horizon line of the attitude indicator.
- Cross check the altimeter and VSI to establish the proper pitch.

4. Return to cruise flight.

- Use the attitude indicator as your primary reference for straight-and-level flight.
- Cross check the airspeed indicator and adjust pitch and power as necessary when you have accelerated to cruise airspeed.

MANEUVER 32 ▪ **Basic Instrument Maneuvers**

CONSTANT AIRSPEED DESCENTS

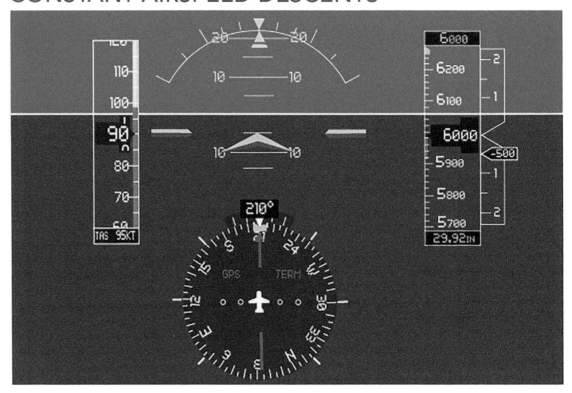

1. Establish the descent attitude.
   - In straight-and-level flight at your desired airspeed, reduce power.
   - Use the airspeed indicator and vertical speed indicator to establish the desired airspeed and climb.
   - Refer to the attitude indicator and heading indicator to maintain directional control.

2. Maintain the descent attitude.
   - Adjust the pitch when you notice changes on the:
     - Attitude indicator.
     - Airspeed indicator.
     - Vertical speed indicator.
   - Adjust the bank when you notice changes on the:
     - Attitude indicator.
     - Heading indicator.
   - Cross check the altimeter to determine your progress toward the desired altitude.

3. Level off at the appropriate point.
   - Refer to the altimeter to begin leveling off at approximately 10 percent of your descent rate above the desired altitude.
   - Adjust the pitch to place the aircraft symbol on the horizon line of the attitude indicator.
   - Cross check the altimeter and VSI to establish the proper pitch.

4. Return to cruise flight.
   - Use the attitude indicator as your primary reference for straight-and-level flight.
   - Cross check the airspeed indicator and adjust pitch and power as necessary when you have accelerated to cruise airspeed.

TURNS TO HEADINGS

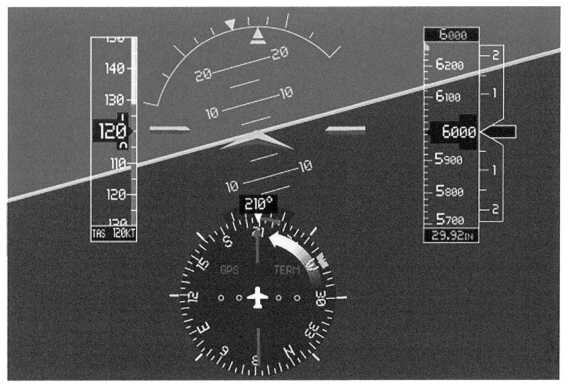

1. Roll into the turn.

    *   Apply coordinated aileron and rudder pressure in the direction of the turn.

    *   Use the attitude indicator to establish the approximate pitch and bank required for a standard rate turn.

> A rule of thumb to determine the approximate bank angle required for a standard-rate turn is to divide your airspeed by 10 and add 1/2 the result. For example, 120 ÷ 10 = 12, 12 + 6 = 18, so 18° is the approximate bank angle required for a standard rate turn at 120 knots. At 80 knots, a standard rate turn requires about a 12° bank angle.

    *   Refer to the turn rate indicator (analog turn coordinator) to verify the standard-rate turn.

    *   Cross check the altimeter and VSI to adjust the pitch as the vertical lift component decreases with an increase in bank.

2. Maintain the turn attitude.

    *   Adjust the pitch when you notice changes on the:
        o   Attitude indicator.
        o   Altimeter.
        o   Vertical speed indicator.
        o   Airspeed indicator.

    *   Adjust the bank when you notice changes on the:
        o   Turn rate indicator.
        o   Attitude indicator.

    *   Cross check the heading indicator to determine your progress.

MANEUVER 32 ▪ **Basic Instrument Maneuvers**

3. Roll out of the turn.
   - Refer to the heading indicator to begin rolling out at approximately 1/2 the angle of bank prior to your heading.
   - Use the attitude indicator as your primary reference for rolling out.
   - Cross check the altimeter to maintain altitude.

RECOVERY FROM UNUSUAL FLIGHT ATTITUDES

Unusual flight attitudes can be a result of many factors such as turbulence, confusion, preoccupation with flight deck duties, carelessness, or a lack of proficiency in basic airplane control. Regardless of the cause of an unusual flight attitude, it usually is unintentional and unexpected. There are two basic scenarios you will practice during your flight training—a nose-high attitude with rapidly decreasing airspeed, and a nose-low attitude with a rapidly increasing airspeed. Learning to recognize and promptly recover from an unusual attitude is a key part of attitude instrument training. Before initiating any recovery, quickly confirm the indications on the attitude indicator are correct by scanning the other instruments.

NOSE-HIGH ATTITUDE

The instrument indications of a nose-high attitude are:
   - A nose-high pitch of the aircraft symbol on the attitude indicator.
   - Rapidly increasing altitude on the altimeter.
   - A high rate of climb on the VSI.
   - Rapidly decreasing airspeed.

> Because a rapid decrease in airspeed can quickly result in a stall, prompt recognition and recovery form a nose-high unusual attitude is essential.

To recover, perform these actions almost simultaneously but in the following sequence.

1. Add power.

2. Lower the nose to place the aircraft symbol on the horizon bar of the attitude indicator.

3. Level the wings using the attitude indicator.

NOSE-LOW ATTITUDE

The instrument indications of a nose-low attitude are:

- A nose-low pitch of the aircraft symbol on the attitude indicator.
- Rapidly decreasing altitude on the altimeter.
- A high rate of descent on the VSI.
- Rapidly increasing airspeed.

To recover, perform these actions almost simultaneously but in the following sequence.

1. Reduce power.

2. Level the wings using the attitude indicator as a reference.

3. Raise the nose to place the aircraft symbol on the horizon bar of the attitude indicator.

> If you attempt to raise the nose before you roll wings level, the increased load factor can result in accelerated stall, a spin, or a force exceeding the airplane's design limits.

MANEUVER 32 ■ **Basic Instrument Maneuvers**

ACS

Basic Instrument Maneuvers

MANEUVER 32 ▪ Basic Instrument Maneuvers

VIII. Basic Instrument Maneuvers

Task	A. Straight-and-Level Flight
References	FAA-H-8083-2, FAA-H-8083-3, FAA-H-8083-15
Objective	To determine that the applicant exhibits satisfactory knowledge, risk management, and skills associated with flying during straight-and-level flight solely by reference to instruments.
Knowledge	The applicant demonstrates understanding of:
PA.VIII.A.K1	Flight instruments as related to:
PA.VIII.A.K1a	a. Sensitivity, limitations, and potential errors in unusual attitudes
PA.VIII.A.K1b	b. Correlation (pitch instruments/bank instruments)
PA.VIII.A.K1c	c. Function and operation
PA.VIII.A.K1d	d. Proper instrument cross-check techniques
Risk Management	The applicant demonstrates the ability to identify, assess and mitigate risks, encompassing:
PA.VIII.A.R1	Instrument flying hazards to include failure to maintain VFR, spatial disorientation, loss of control, fatigue, stress, and emergency off airport landings.
PA.VIII.A.R2	Failure to seek assistance or declare an emergency in a deteriorating situation.
PA.VIII.A.R3	Collision hazards, to include aircraft, terrain, obstacles, and wires.
PA.VIII.A.R4	Distractions, loss of situational awareness, and/or improper task management.
Skills	The applicant demonstrates the ability to:
PA.VIII.A.S1	Maintain straight-and-level flight using proper instrument cross-check and interpretation, and coordinated control application.
PA.VIII.A.S2	Maintain altitude ±200 feet, heading ±20°, and airspeed ±10 knots.

VIII. Basic Instrument Maneuvers

Task	B. Constant Airspeed Climbs
References	FAA-H-8083-2, FAA-H-8083-3, FAA-H-8083-15
Objective	To determine that the applicant exhibits satisfactory knowledge, risk management, and skills associated with attitude instrument flying during constant airspeed climbs solely by reference to instruments.
Knowledge	The applicant demonstrates understanding of:
PA.VIII.B.K1	Flight instruments as related to:
PA.VIII.B.K1a	a. Sensitivity, limitations, and potential errors in unusual attitudes
PA.VIII.B.K1b	b. Correlation (pitch instruments/bank instruments)
PA.VIII.B.K1c	c. Function and operation
PA.VIII.B.K1d	d. Proper instrument cross-check techniques
Risk Management	The applicant demonstrates the ability to identify, assess and mitigate risks, encompassing:
PA.VIII.B.R1	Instrument flying hazards to include failure to maintain VFR, spatial disorientation, loss of control, fatigue, stress, and emergency off airport landings.
PA.VIII.B.R2	Failure to seek assistance or declare an emergency in a deteriorating situation.
PA.VIII.B.R3	Collision hazards, to include aircraft, terrain, obstacles, and wires.
PA.VIII.B.R4	Distractions, loss of situational awareness, and/or improper task management.
Skills	The applicant demonstrates the ability to:
PA.VIII.B.S1	Transition to the climb pitch attitude and power setting on an assigned heading using proper instrument cross-check and interpretation, and coordinated flight control application.
PA.VIII.B.S2	Demonstrate climbs at a constant airspeed to specific altitudes in straight flight and turns.
PA.VIII.B.S3	Level off at the assigned altitude and maintain altitude ±200 feet, heading ±20°, and airspeed ±10 knots.

VIII. Basic Instrument Maneuvers

Task	C. Constant Airspeed Descents
References	FAA-H-8083-2, FAA-H-8083-3, FAA-H-8083-15
Objective	To determine that the applicant exhibits satisfactory knowledge, risk management, and skills associated with attitude instrument flying during constant airspeed descents solely by reference to instruments.
Knowledge	The applicant demonstrates understanding of:
PA.VIII.C.K1	Flight instruments as related to:
PA.VIII.C.K1a	a. Sensitivity, limitations, and potential errors in unusual attitudes
PA.VIII.C.K1b	b. Correlation (pitch instruments/bank instruments)
PA.VIII.C.K1c	c. Function and operation
PA.VIII.C.K1d	d. Proper instrument cross-check techniques
Risk Management	The applicant demonstrates the ability to identify, assess and mitigate risks, encompassing:
PA.VIII.C.R1	Instrument flying hazards to include failure to maintain VFR, spatial disorientation, loss of control, fatigue, stress, and emergency off airport landings.
PA.VIII.C.R2	Failure to seek assistance or declare an emergency in a deteriorating situation.
PA.VIII.C.R3	Collision hazards, to include aircraft, terrain, obstacles, and wires.
PA.VIII.C.R4	Distractions, loss of situational awareness, and/or improper task management.
Skills	The applicant demonstrates the ability to:
PA.VIII.C.S1	Transition to the descent pitch attitude and power setting on an assigned heading using proper instrument cross-check and interpretation, and coordinated flight control application.
PA.VIII.C.S2	Demonstrate descents at a constant airspeed to specific altitudes in straight flight and turns.
PA.VIII.C.S3	Level off at the assigned altitude and maintain altitude ±200 feet, heading ±20°, and airspeed ±10 knots.

VIII. Basic Instrument Maneuvers

Task	D. Turns to Headings
References	FAA-H-8083-2, FAA-H-8083-3, FAA-H-8083-15
Objective	To determine that the applicant exhibits satisfactory knowledge, risk management, and skills associated with attitude instrument flying during turns to headings solely by reference to instruments.
Knowledge	The applicant demonstrates understanding of:
PA.VIII.D.K1	Flight instruments as related to:
PA.VIII.D.K1a	a. Sensitivity, limitations, and potential errors in unusual attitudes
PA.VIII.D.K1b	b. Correlation (pitch instruments/bank instruments)
PA.VIII.D.K1c	c. Function and operation
PA.VIII.D.K1d	d. Proper instrument cross-check techniques
Risk Management	The applicant demonstrates the ability to identify, assess and mitigate risks, encompassing:
PA.VIII.D.R1	Instrument flying hazards to include failure to maintain VFR, spatial disorientation, loss of control, fatigue, stress, and emergency off airport landings.
PA.VIII.D.R2	Failure to seek assistance or declare an emergency in a deteriorating situation.
PA.VIII.D.R3	Collision hazards, to include aircraft, terrain, obstacles, and wires.
PA.VIII.D.R4	Distractions, loss of situational awareness, and/or improper task management.
Skills	The applicant demonstrates the ability to:
PA.VIII.D.S1	Demonstrate turns to headings, maintain altitude ±200 feet, maintain a standard rate turn, roll out on the assigned heading ±10°, and maintain airspeed ±10 knots.

MANEUVER 32 ■ Basic Instrument Maneuvers

VIII. Basic Instrument Maneuvers

Task	E. *Recovery from Unusual Flight Attitudes*
References	FAA-H-8083-2, FAA-H-8083-3, FAA-H-8083-15
Objective	To determine that the applicant exhibits satisfactory knowledge, risk management, and skills associated with attitude instrument flying while recovering from unusual attitudes solely by reference to instruments.
Knowledge	The applicant demonstrates understanding of:
PA.VIII.E.K1	Flight instruments as related to:
PA.VIII.E.K1a	a. Sensitivity, limitations, and potential errors in unusual attitudes
PA.VIII.E.K1b	b. Correlation (pitch instruments/bank instruments)
PA.VIII.E.K1c	c. Function and operation
PA.VIII.E.K1d	d. Proper instrument cross-check techniques
Risk Management	The applicant demonstrates the ability to identify, assess and mitigate risks, encompassing:
PA.VIII.E.R1	Instrument flying hazards to include failure to maintain VFR, spatial disorientation, loss of control, fatigue, stress, and emergency off airport landings.
PA.VIII.E.R2	Failure to seek assistance or declare an emergency in a deteriorating situation.
PA.VIII.E.R3	Collision hazards, to include aircraft, terrain, obstacles, and wires.
PA.VIII.E.R4	Distractions, loss of situational awareness, and/or improper task management.
PA.VIII.E.R5	Failure to interpret flight instruments.
PA.VIII.E.R6	Failure to unload the wings in recovering from high G situations.
Skills	The applicant demonstrates the ability to:
PA.VIII.E.S1	Recognize unusual flight attitudes; perform the correct, coordinated, and smooth flight control application to resolve unusual pitch and bank attitudes while staying within the airplane's limitations and flight parameters.

MANEUVER 32 ■ **Basic Instrument Maneuvers**

33 — Night Operations

In many respects, night flying is more pleasant than daytime flying. At night, the air is generally smoother and cooler, which results in a more comfortable flight and better airplane performance. In addition, at night you normally experience less airport traffic and less congestion on communication frequencies. To become proficient at night operations, you must consider factors that affect preparing for and performing a night flight. In addition to the procedures discussed here, refer to the Jeppesen *Private Pilot* textbook for more information about night flying and the associated physiological aspects.

PREPARING FOR A NIGHT FLIGHT

Although comprehensive planning for any flight is essential, preparation for a night flight is inherently more detailed. You must consider a variety of factors that are specific to night flying and assess your abilities and limitations prior to flying at night.

FLIGHT PLANNING

Although your flight planning process is basically the same as for a day flight, you must take some additional actions when planning a night flight:

- Use flight information sources, such as aeronautical charts, the Airport/Facility Directory section of the Chart Supplement and NOTAMs to check the availability and status of enroute and destination airport lighting.

- Use an electronic flight bag (EFB) for flight planning so your course is easy to see or draw course lines in black to be more distinguishable on paper charts.

- Select visual checkpoints that are prominently lighted, such as airport rotating beacons, lighted obstructions, city or town lights, and major highways.

- Plan to use GPS or other radio navigation aids.

- Make a No-Go decision if a chance of marginal VFR conditions exists. Consider canceling the flight if the temperature/dewpoint spread is close, which indicates possible ground fog formation.

- Pay close attention to wind direction and speed because airplane drift is substantially more difficult to detect during takeoffs and landings at night.

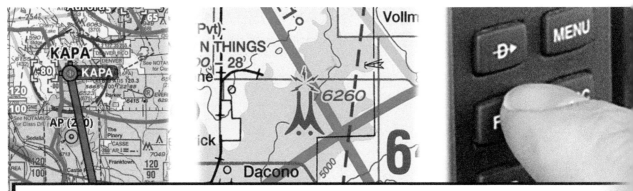

!PUB 05/042 Pueblo Memorial, Pueblo, CO (KPUB) Runway 17 runway end ID light out of service May 31, 2018 2108Z to Jun 21, 2018 2359Z

PREFLIGHT

Become thoroughly familiar with the airplane's flight deck, instrumentation, and control layout so you can locate hard-to-see equipment in low light conditions. Be aware that your eyes take at least 30 minutes to adapt to the darkness. Make sure you have a reliable flashlight for the preflight inspection and an in-cabin flashlight to read charts or to use in the event of an electrical malfunction. Organize and place your flashlight, EFB, charts, pencil, and other necessities in an easily accessible location.

> If you are flying an older airplane that has fuses, you must ensure that a spare set is available.

Take these actions when performing a preflight inspection at night:

- Check the airplane in a well-lighted area or plan for an earlier departure so that you can complete your preflight inspection before dark.
- Check the cabin and instrument panel flood, post, or internal lights for proper illumination.

> The instruments and instrument panel might be lighted in one of several ways.
> - Flood—a single centrally-mounted light with a rheostat to regulate the intensity.
> - Post—a light source adjacent to and directed at each instrument and shaded from your vision.
> - Internal—a light source located inside the instrument, such as the magnetic compass and the radios.

- Check the exterior airplane lights (position, anticollision, landing, and taxi lights) for proper illumination and lens condition. Tap the lenses, if practical, to check for loose connections.

> To conserve battery power, turn on the lights only long enough to verify proper operation. Some airplanes have small plastic attachments on the wing tips which reflect light so you can check the operation of the position lights from the flight deck.
>
> When operating the landing and taxi lights, avoid shining them in the direction of a taxiing aircraft to prevent impairing another pilot's night vision.

- To prevent a mishap during taxi, check the surrounding ramp area for hazards such as tie-down ropes, chocks, and stepladders.

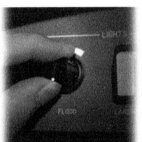

MANEUVER 33 ▪ **Night Operations**

PERFORMING A NIGHT FLIGHT

Due to limited visibility and illusions created by low light conditions, night airport operations can be very different than those you are accustomed to during daytime. Ensure you are familiar with the lighting systems used for airports, runways, obstructions, and other visual aids at night. Refer to the Jeppesen *Private Pilot* textbook and the *Aeronautical Information Manual (AIM)* for lighting descriptions.

ENGINE START, TAXI, AND BEFORE TAKEOFF

Take these actions when starting the engine, taxiing, and performing the before takeoff check at night.

- Turn on the anticollision lights and flash the position lights to warn others of engine start.
- Use the taxi and landing light as necessary during taxi but turn these lights off if they might blind other pilots.

> Wait until you are actually ready to taxi before you turn on the taxi light.

- Taxi slower at night, especially in congested ramp areas.

> Because taxi and landing lights usually cast a beam which is narrow and concentrated, illumination to the side of the airplane is minimal. After you are in runup area, turn the taxi and landing lights off until your runup is complete.

- Maintain constant brake pressure when performing the Before Takeoff checklist and stay alert for any unintentional movement.

> You can usually detect any unintended forward movement of the airplane during the day. However, the airplane might creep forward at night without you noticing.

TAKEOFF AND CLIMB

Although the procedure for night takeoffs is the same as for day takeoffs, many of the normal outside visual cues are unavailable. To compensate for this, take these actions when performing a takeoff and climb at night:

- Adjust the flight deck lights as low as possible to enable you to see references outside the airplane but still be able to read the instruments.
- Turn on the landing and taxi lights.
- Check the flight instruments frequently to ensure that you maintain the proper pitch attitude, heading, and airspeed.
- During initial climb, in addition to using outside visual references, maintain a normal climb attitude on the attitude indicator and cross check the VSI, altimeter, and airspeed indicator.

The first 500 feet of altitude gain after takeoff is considered to be a critical period because you are transitioning from the comparatively well-lighted airport area into what sometimes appears as total darkness.

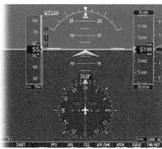

NAVIGATION

Navigation at night is usually fairly simple because the outlines of major cities and towns are clearly discernible. With sufficient altitude, major metropolitan areas are visible during favorable weather from distances up to 100 miles or more. Major highways tend to stand out at night because of the presence of numerous automobile headlights. Less traveled roads are usually not so easy to see, unless the moonlight is bright enough to illuminate them. On clear, moonlit nights, outlines of the terrain and other surface features are dimly visible. For example, you can often discern the outlines of bodies of water by noting the reflection of the moonlight. However, on extremely dark nights, terrain features are nearly invisible, except in brightly lighted, populated areas.

After you have taken off and reached a safe altitude, take these actions to maintain orientation and navigate at night:

- To preserve your night vision, reduce the level of cabin light or use an in-cabin flashlight for reading paper charts. Turn down the brightness on integrated displays and use night or color inversion settings to view charts and documents on EFBs.

Color inversion features invert white and black elements to reduce the glare of charts and documents for night viewing.

- Use off-center viewing to scan for traffic.

Due to the reduction in outside visual references, you might have a tendency to spend too much time looking at the flight instruments. Therefore, you must make a special effort to scan for traffic.

- When scanning for traffic, interpret the position light relationships of other aircraft to determine their direction of flight.
- To prevent inadvertently flying into clouds or deteriorating weather, continually update your weather briefing with by using data link weather services and Flight Service.

Use caution with regard to relying on data link weather products, especially those related to quickly-developing and fast-moving convective weather. NEXRAD data can, in rare cases, be as much as 20 minutes older than the age indicated on the cockpit display.

- Maintain a high cruising altitude to keep the airplane well above terrain and obstacles and to increase gliding distance in the event of an engine failure.

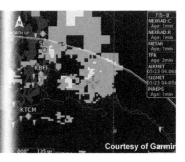

Courtesy of Garmin

MANEUVER 33 ■ **Night Operations**

TRAFFIC PATTERN AND LANDING

Many pilots have a tendency to fly higher or lower approaches at night than during the daytime. Therefore, carefully consider traffic pattern procedures and the factors that enable you to maintain the proper descent angle on final approach. To become proficient landing at night you will practice with and without the landing light. Take these actions to perform a traffic pattern and landing at night:

- Because it can be difficult to ascertain the runway layout at night, fly toward the airport beacon until you can distinguish the runway lights.

> You can easily locate airports that are away from congested areas by the lights outlining the runways. You might find it difficult to identify airports near or within large cities because the airport lights tend to blend with the city lights. Know the exact location of an airport relative to the city and the characteristics of its lighting pattern.

- Fly a normal traffic pattern and approach, being sure to cross check the altimeter and VSI to maintain the rate of descent.
- Use visual glideslope indicators if available, for descent angle guidance.
- Use the runway lights as a peripheral cue for beginning the flare, being aware that runway lights seem to rise and spread laterally as you near the touchdown point,
- Continue a constant approach descent until the landing light reflects on the runway and you can clearly see tire marks.

> It is standard operating procedure to use your landing lights for night landings, even though they might cause an illusion of runway height. The portion of the runway illuminated by the landing lights seems higher than the surrounding area, potentially leading to a high flare. In addition, focusing your attention on the area immediately in front of the airplane is poor practice even though the arrangement of most landing lights tends to encourage this technique. When using landing lights, your sighting point should be near the forward limit of the lighted area.

Although you will perform most of your night landings using landing lights, you should also practice landings without the aid of the landing lights. During no-light landings, you should begin your flare when the runway lights at the far end of the runway first appear to be rising higher than the airplane. This technique demands a smooth and timely flare using power and pitch changes as necessary for the airplane to settle softly on the runway.

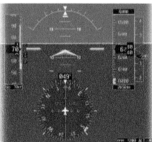

NIGHT EMERGENCIES

When flying at night, especially during a night cross-country, high cruising altitudes provide an improved margin of safety. Typically at a higher altitude, range is increased, the airplane is well above normal obstructions, and gliding distance is greater in the event of engine failure. For example, at 10,000 feet AGL, a light airplane with a glide ratio of 8 to 1 might glide 13 miles. This distance might place the airplane within range of an airport.

ENGINE FAILURE

Take these actions to manage an engine failure and perform an emergency landing at night:

- Maintain control and use the same AFM/POH-recommended procedures as for daytime emergency landings.

- Select a landing area close to public access if possible.

> You can use a highway as an emergency landing site at night, but you must exercise extreme caution to avoid power lines and vehicular traffic.

- If you are familiar with the condition of the surrounding terrain, turn toward an unlighted area to avoid structures.

- Turn on the landing light during the final approach to illuminate the terrain and any obstacles.

Pilot's Operating Handbook

3.5 EMERGENCY LANDINGS

3.5.1 EMERGENCY LANDING WITH ENGINE OFF
1. Select suitable landing area. If no level landing area is available, a landing on an upward slope should be sought.
2. Consider wind.
3. Approach: If possible, fly along a short-cut rectangular circuit. On the downwind leg of the circuit the landing area should be inspected for obstacles from a suitable height. The degree of offset at each part of the circuit will allow the wind speed and direction to be assessed.
4. Airspeed .... 73 KIAS (1150 kg, 2535 lb.)
                                    68 KIAS (1000 kg, 2205 lb.)

INADVERTENT ENTRY INTO IMC AT NIGHT

A major safety concern for non-instrument rated pilots flying at night is unintentional flight into instrument meteorological conditions (IMC), also referred to as IFR conditions. The risk of flying into an overcast increases at night because seeing the clouds is difficult. Before you fly at night, obtain a thorough weather briefing. Give special attention to any information in the weather briefing that indicates possible formation of clouds, fog, or precipitation.

If you do penetrate IMC, calmly, but immediately, reference your flight instruments to initiate a 180° standard-rate turn to fly out of the weather conditions. Indications that you might be entering IMC at night include:

- A disappearance of lights on the ground or stars in the sky.

- A halo or luminous glow around position lights or a reflection of the landing and anticollision lights.

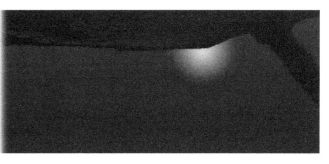

XI. Night Operations

Task	A. Night Preparation
References	FAA-H-8083-2, FAA-H-8083-3, FAA-H-8083-25; AIM; POH/AFM
Objective	To determine that the applicant exhibits satisfactory knowledge, risk management, and skills associated with night operations.
Knowledge	The applicant demonstrates understanding of:
PA.XI.A.K1	Physiological aspects of vision related to night flying.
PA.XI.A.K2	Lighting systems identifying airports, runways, taxiways and obstructions, as well as pilot controlled lighting.
PA.XI.A.K3	Airplane equipment and lighting requirements for night operations.
PA.XI.A.K4	Personal equipment essential for night flight.
PA.XI.A.K5	Night orientation, navigation, and chart reading techniques.
Risk Management	The applicant demonstrates the ability to identify, assess and mitigate risks, encompassing:
PA.XI.A.R1	Collision hazards, to include aircraft, terrain, obstacles, and wires.
PA.XI.A.R2	Distractions, loss of situational awareness, and/or improper task management.
PA.XI.A.R3	Hazards specific to night flying.
Skills	*N/A* **Note:** *Not generally evaluated in flight. If the practical test is conducted at night, all ACS Tasks are evaluated in that environment, thus there is no need for explicit Task elements to exist here.*

MANEUVER 33 ▪ **Night Operations**

EXERCISES — SPECIAL FLIGHT OPERATIONS

30 — BASIC INSTRUMENT MANEUVERS

1. What instrument replaces the natural horizon during instrument flight?

_____

2. What is the radial cross-check?

_____

3. What is the four-step process for maintaining and changing attitudes when practicing attitude instrument flying?

_____

_____

_____

_____

4. True/False. A tight grip on the control wheel/stick ensures smooth and precise attitude control.

5. During a constant airspeed climb, what action should you take to counteract the effect of P-factor?

_____

6. Typically, at what altitude would you begin your level-off if your target altitude is 2,000 feet, and your rate of descent is 500 feet per minute?_____

7. What is the approximate angle of bank that will result in a standard-rate turn for an airspeed of 100 knots? _____

8. What instrument should be referenced to confirm and maintain a standard-rate turn?

_____

9. What are the three steps to recover from a nose-high unusual attitude?

_____

10. When recovering from a nose-low unusual attitude, why should you level the wings before applying back pressure on the control wheel/stick?

_____

31 — NIGHT OPERATIONS

1. Name at least two actions you should take when planning a night flight.

   _____

   _____

2. Why is it important to taxi slower at night than during the day?

   _____

3. True/False. During takeoff, adjust the flight deck lights to full brightness to enable you easily read the instruments.

4. Name at two actions you should take when performing a traffic pattern and landing at night.

   _____

   _____

5. What are two indications that at you might be entering IMC at night?

   _____

   _____

6. What action should you take if you inadvertently fly into IMC at night?

   _____

ANSWERS

GROUND OPERATIONS

1 — PREFLIGHT INSPECTION

1. You should check the aircraft logbooks and records to ensure that the appropriate airworthiness directives have been complied with, maintenance requirements have been met, and aircraft inspections have been performed.

2. **A**irworthiness certificate; **R**egistration certificate; **R**adio station class license (if applicable); **O**perating limitations, which may be in the form of an FAA-approved airplane flight manual and/or pilot's operating handbook (AFM/POH), placards, instrument markings, or any combination thereof; **W**eight and balance data, including the equipment list

3. Because it is heavier than fuel, water settles to the bottom of the tester.

4. True

5. A

2 — ENGINE STARTING

1. False

2. C

3. In cold weather—when air temperatures are below 20°F (-6°C)—the AFM/POH typically recommends using an external preheater and/or an external power source to start the engine.

4. 60 seconds

5. Immediately shut down the engine to prevent possible damage.

3 — TAXIING

1. False

2. Decrease

3. Apply the brakes in the direction of the turn.

4. Fully turn the control wheel/stick to the left, placing the left aileron in the up position. Hold the control wheel/stick to maintain a neutral elevator position.

5. Fully turn the control wheel/stick to the left, placing the left aileron in the up position. Hold the control wheel/stick full forward to maintain the elevator/stabilator in the full down position.

4 — BEFORE TAKEOFF CHECK

1. Position the airplane so the propeller blast is not directed toward other aircraft, buildings, or vehicles. If possible, point the nose of the airplane into the wind to improve engine cooling. To prevent damage to the propeller and other parts of the airplane, avoid engine runups on loose gravel or sand.

2. True

3. C

4. Verify that indications for items, such as oil temperature, oil pressure, fuel flow, vacuum pressure, and electrical charge, register in the green arc/sector.

5. 1200

5 — POSTFLIGHT PROCEDURES

1. C
2. Actions in the engine shutdown checklist normally include:
   - Set the parking brake.
   - Set the power to idle, or as recommended by the manufacturer.
   - Turn off all electrical equipment.
   - Turn off the avionics power switch.
   - Set the mixture control to LEAN (IDLE CUTOFF)
   - Turn the ignition switch off when the engine stops. As an added precaution, remove the key from the ignition.
   - Turn the master switch off.
   - Install the control lock.
   - Record the flight time.
3. False
4. At the rib locations
5. During a postflight inspection you should check for oil and fuel streaks on the cowling, fuel stains under the wings, damage to the landing gear and tires, such as flat spots, and leaking hydraulic fluid near the brakes.

BASIC MANEUVERS

6 — STRAIGHT-AND-LEVEL FLIGHT

1. The natural horizon to the front and sides of your airplane.
2. Focusing outside the flight deck helps you see and avoid other aircraft.
3. True
4. C
5. Cross check the flight instruments

7 — CLIMBS

1. Best angle-of-climb speed (V_X)
2. Best rate-of-climb speed (V_Y)
3. False
4. Decrease
5. 10%

8 — DESCENTS

1. True
2. Higher
3. 4,050 feet
4. True
5. Raise the nose

9 — TURNS

1. Shallow—less than 20°; medium—20° to 45°; steep—45° or more
2. False
3. How long you deflect the ailerons
4. 075°
5. Add power

AIRPORT OPERATIONS

10 — NORMAL TAKEOFF AND CLIMB

1. Apply right rudder.
2. Keep your hand on the throttle throughout the takeoff to ensure that the throttle does not slide back during the takeoff roll. You will also be able to reduce power to idle quickly if you decide to reject the takeoff.
3. The airplane can be forced into the air prematurely and then settle back to the runway. Also, the airplane might be at such a high angle of attack that it cannot accelerate to climb speed.
4. The standard procedure for departing an uncontrolled airport is to fly straight out or to make a 45° turn in the direction of the traffic pattern.
5. Reject the takeoff by reducing the power to idle, maintaining directional control with the rudder pedals, and applying brakes.

11 — CROSSWIND TAKEOFF AND CLIMB

1. Refer to your airplane's AFM/POH.
2. False
3. Decrease
4. The airplane tracks straight down the runway and you feel no side load on the landing gear.
5. Enter a crab—turn the nose into the wind to offset the crosswind, level the wings, and adjust the rudder pressure to maintain runway alignment.

12 — TRAFFIC PATTERNS

1. Downwind, base, final, departure, and crosswind
2. True
3. 10 miles
4. If you are unfamiliar with the airport and cannot obtain information from a UNICOM operator, control tower, or automated weather station, overfly the airport at least 500 feet above the traffic pattern altitude to determine the landing runway and the associated pattern direction. Use visual indicators such as the segmented circle, wind direction indicator, landing direction indicator, or traffic pattern indicator.
5. *"Front Range traffic, Piper 9163 Kilo, final, Runway 26, touch-and-go, Boulder."*

13 — NORMAL APPROACH AND LANDING

1. False
2. The position abeam the intended landing area
3. Reduce power, extend flaps, or both.
4. Add power and decrease the pitch attitude slightly.
5. Flare, touchdown, and roll-out
6. Your heels should be on the floor so there is no tendency to use the brakes inadvertently. Braking on touchdown with the wheels spinning at a fast rate can cause flat spots on the tires.
7. Excess airspeed and/or excess power

14 — FORWARD SLIP

1. A forward slip is used to steepen the airplane's descent angle to dissipate altitude without increasing the airspeed.

2. False

3. To establish the slip attitude: reduce power to idle and establish a glide toward the runway or landing area. Use the control wheel/stick to lower one wing. Apply opposite rudder to keep the airplane from turning in the direction of the lowered wing. To prevent the airspeed from increasing, raise the nose slightly above the normal gliding position.

15 — GO-AROUND

1. Reasons for performing a go around include:
   - You have not established a stabilized approach on final
   - The airplane has not touched down in the first third of the runway
   - An animal, aircraft or vehicle is on the runway.
   - You encounter wind shear or wake turbulence on final approach.
   - You perform a faulty landing.
   - ATC instructs you to do so.

2. Apply power.

3. B

16 — CROSSWIND APPROACH AND LANDING

1. Crab method; wing-low (sideslip) method

2. Start your turn to final sooner and/or use up to 30° of bank.

3. C

4. Perform a go-around and land on a runway with more favorable wind conditions.

5. Increase

EMERGENCY OPERATIONS

17 — SYSTEMS AND EQUIPMENT MALFUNCTIONS

1. Actions to take if experience a partial power loss include:
   - Follow the checklist in your AFM/POH to troubleshoot and restore power.
   - If you are unable to restore power, decide how to proceed based on the cause of the power loss, the power available, airplane performance, and the flight environment.
   - If the airplane can maintain altitude or climb, you might be able to continue the flight to a nearby airport in a reduced power condition.
   - If your airplane's performance with partial power is not sufficient to maintain altitude or the cause of the power loss is severe enough that an engine failure is imminent, consider performing an off-airport precautionary landing.
   - Update your choice of landing options, and be prepared to perform an emergency approach and landing.

2. Actions to take if the airplane's alternator fails include:
   - Determine the essential electrical equipment for the flight and severity of the situation based on factors such as VFR or IFR conditions, day or night, and distance from an airport.
   - Shed electrical load to preserve battery power for essential equipment.
   - Notify ATC of the situation and use ATC services, such as radar vectors, as appropriate.
   - Be prepared to control the airplane and land without electrical equipment.

3. Three factors to consider when performing a no-flap approach and landing are:

- The glide path is not as steep as with flaps extended, so the higher nose attitude on final can cause errors in your judgment of height and distance.
- Landing distance is substantially increased.
- Floating during the flare is likely.

4. Managing smoke or fire in the cabin typically involves these actions:

- Turn off the master switch to remove the possible source of the fire.
- If flames exist, use the fire extinguisher to put out the fire.
- After extinguishing the fire, open the air vents to clear the cabin of smoke and fumes.
- Land as soon as possible.

5. Maintain control of the airplane, then land as soon as practical and secure the door.

18 — EMERGENCY DESCENT

1. An emergency descent is a maneuver for descending to a lower altitude as rapidly as possible within the structural limitations of the airplane. You might need to perform an emergency descent due to an uncontrollable fire, smoke in the cockpit, a sudden loss of cabin pressurization, or any other situation that demands an immediate rapid descent.

2. C

3. Bank approximately 30° to 45° to maintain a positive load factor on the airplane and increase the rate of descent. Turning also helps you scan for traffic below and look for a possible emergency landing site.

4. Maneuvering speed (V_A)

5. 3,100 feet MSL

19 — EMERGENCY APPROACH AND LANDING

1. Maintain control of the airplane and adjust the pitch to achieve best glide speed.

2. False

3. When selecting a field, you must consider the wind direction and speed, length of the field, obstructions, and surface condition

4. False

5. 7700

6. Extending the flaps shortens the glide distance.

7. Three steps to follow if an engine failure occurs immediately after takeoff are:

- Reduce the pitch attitude. Lower the nose and pitch for best glide speed.
- If time permits, follow the steps on the emergency checklist. Perform memory tasks to restart the engine, such as enriching the mixture or turning on the auxiliary fuel pump.
- Land straight ahead. Extend the flaps as necessary. Make only small heading changes to avoid obstacles.

8. An attempt to turn back to the runway in the event of an engine failure after takeoff greatly increases your risk of an accident because:

- You have insufficient altitude to complete a turn considering the radius and rate of descent.
- A steep turn increases the descent rate and stall speed, which is particularly dangerous at slow speeds close to the ground.
- A cross-control stall situation can develop if you add excessive rudder to increase the turn rate and add aileron control in the opposite direction to counter the increasing bank angle.

FLIGHT MANEUVERS

20 — SLOW FLIGHT

1. For the practical test, the Private Pilot Airman Certification Standards (ACS) state that you should "establish and maintain an airspeed at which any further increase in angle of attack, increase in load factor, or reduction in power would result in a stall warning (e.g. aircraft buffet, stall horn, etc.)."

2. 1,500 feet AGL

3. B

4. True

5. Retract the flaps in increments.

21 — POWER-OFF STALLS

1. In the landing configuration

2. 5 to 10 knots before the stall

3. The stall definitions are:
   - Impending stall—a buffet or aural warning is triggered but the wings have not reached the critical angle of attack.
   - Full stall—the critical angle of attack is exceeded. Indications of a full stall are typically an uncommanded nose-down pitch that can be combined with an uncommanded rolling motion.

4. Release back pressure to reduce the angle of attack. Level the wings (if necessary) using coordinated aileron and rudder pressure. Add full power, and set the carburetor heat to COLD (if applicable). Retract the flaps to an intermediate setting.

5. A shallow-banked turn (up to 20° bank angle)

22 — POWER-ON STALLS

1. During takeoffs and departure climbs

2. In the takeoff configuration

3. B

4. As you reach liftoff speed, simultaneously set takeoff power (or the recommended climb power setting) and smoothly apply back pressure on the control wheel/stick to raise the airplane's nose to an attitude that will induce a stall. Maintain the pitch attitude until a full stall occurs. Ensure you maintain coordinated flight.

5. Decrease

23 — DEMONSTRATED STALLS

1. False

2. You pitch up too quickly during a stall recovery before the airplane reaches sufficient flying speed.

3. An accelerated stall occurs at a higher-than-normal airspeed in steep turns, pullups, or other abrupt changes in flight attitude. The stalls that occur from these types of maneuvers tend to develop faster than normal unaccelerated stalls.

4. A cross-control stall is most likely to occur in the traffic pattern during a turn from the base leg to final approach when trying to compensate for overshooting the extended runway centerline.

5. You perform a go-around and let the airplane pitch up to a stall attitude because the trim is set for landing, or you perform a takeoff with excessive nose-up trim.

6. Reduce the power to idle. Moving the throttle to idle will eliminate thrust and minimize the altitude loss.

24 — STEEP TURNS

1. 45°

2. Left turn

3. Decrease the angle of bank first, then increase back pressure on the control wheel to raise the nose. After you regain your desired altitude, roll back to the desired angle of bank.

4. 20°

5. True

GROUND REFERENCE MANEUVERS

25 — RECTANGULAR COURSE

1. Traffic pattern

2. Clear the area for traffic and check to ensure there are no obstructions such as towers or power lines. Also, select an emergency landing area within gliding distance.

3. 45°

4. Abeam the crosswind segment of the field boundary

5. The turn from the upwind leg to the crosswind leg

26 — S-TURNS

1. The ground reference line should be oriented perpendicular, or 90°, to the wind direction.

2. False

3. Your groundspeed will decrease.

4. When flying from a tailwind to a headwind, the groundspeed decreases. Therefore, you should also decrease the bank angle as the turn progresses. In this way, the ground track will be a uniform semicircle.

5. When crossing the reference line.

27 — TURNS AROUND A POINT

1. An intersection of roads or fence lines is more desirable, because the wing might momentarily block your view of the reference point during the maneuver. By selecting a road or fence line intersection, you can mentally project these lines to their logical intersection and maintain your orientation..

2. Enter the maneuver downwind.

3. 45°

4. When headed directly downwind

5. When headed directly upwind

PERFORMANCE TAKEOFFS AND LANDINGS

28 — SHORT-FIELD TAKEOFF AND CLIMB

1. The usable runway length is short and/or the runway available for takeoff is restricted by obstructions at the departure end.

2. 50 feet

3. False

4. This procedure enables you to determine that the engine is functioning properly before you take off from a field where power availability is critical and distance to abort a takeoff is limited.

5. A premature nose-high attitude produces more drag and results in a longer takeoff roll. In addition, if the airplane lifts off too soon, it can stall, settle back to the runway, or hit the obstacle.

29 — SHORT-FIELD APPROACH AND LANDINGS

1. When there is a relatively short landing area and/or when an approach must be made over obstacles that limit the available landing area.

2. Steeper

3. Full flaps allow a steeper descent angle without increasing airspeed.

4. True

5. An excessive amount of airspeed can cause the airplane to touch down too far beyond the runway threshold and exceed the available landing area during roll-out.

30 — SOFT-FIELD TAKEOFF AND CLIMB

1. To transfer the weight of the airplane from the landing gear to the wings as quickly and smoothly as possible to eliminate drag caused by surfaces such as tall grass, soft dirt, or snow

2. Apply full back pressure on the control wheel/stick to reduce weight on the nosewheel while taxiing.

3. False

4. The airplane can assume an extremely nose-high attitude, which can cause the tail skid to come in contact with the runway.

5. Allow the airplane to accelerate in ground effect to V_X or V_Y (as appropriate).

31 — SOFT-FIELD APPROACH AND LANDING

1. To ease the weight of the airplane from the wings to the main landing gear as gently and slowly as possible, keeping the nosewheel off the soft surface during most of the landing roll

2. To allow the airplane to touch down at a minimum speed

3. To dissipate forward speed

4. False

5. C

SPECIAL FLIGHT OPERATIONS

32 — BASIC INSTRUMENT MANEUVERS

1. The attitude indicator

2. The radial cross-check is a scan pattern during which you spend 80 to 90 percent of flight time looking at the attitude indicator and taking only quick glances at the other flight instruments.

3. The four-step process for maintaining and changing attitudes when practicing attitude instrument flying is: 1) Establish the attitude; 2) Trim to relieve control pressures; 3) Cross check to verify the attitude; 4) Adjust for deviations.

4. False

5. Apply right rudder as necessary to control the left-turning tendency.

6. 2,050 feet

7. 15°

8. Turn rate indicator/turn coordinator

9. To recover from a nose-high unusual attitude, perform these actions almost simultaneously but in the following sequence: 1) Add power; 2) Lower the nose to place the aircraft symbol on the horizon bar of the attitude indicator; 3) Level the wings using the attitude indicator.

10. If you attempt to raise the nose before you roll wings level, the increased load factor can result in accelerated stall, a spin, or a force exceeding the airplane's design limits.

33 — NIGHT OPERATIONS

1. Additional actions you should take when planning a night flight:
   - Use flight information sources, such as aeronautical charts, the Airport/Facility Directory section of the Chart Supplement and NOTAMs to check the availability and status of enroute and destination airport lighting.
   - Use an electronic flight bag (EFB) for flight planning so your course is easy to see or draw course lines in black to be more distinguishable on paper charts.
   - Select visual checkpoints that are prominently lighted, such as airport rotating beacons, lighted obstructions, city or town lights, and major highways.
   - Plan to use GPS or other radio navigation aids.
   - Make a No-Go decision if a chance of marginal VFR conditions exists. Consider canceling the flight if the temperature/dewpoint spread is close, which indicates possible ground fog formation.
   - Pay close attention to wind direction and speed because airplane drift is substantially more difficult to detect during takeoffs and landings at night.

2. Because the narrow beam of the taxi light does not illuminate the areas to the left and right of the airplane.

3. False

4. Actions you should take when performing a traffic pattern and landing at night include:
   - Because it can be difficult to ascertain the runway layout at night, fly toward the airport beacon until you can distinguish the runway lights.
   - Fly a normal traffic pattern and approach, being sure to cross check the altimeter and VSI to maintain the rate of descent.
   - Use visual glideslope indicators if available, for descent angle guidance.
   - Use the runway lights as a peripheral cue for beginning the flare, being aware that runway lights seem to rise and spread laterally as you near the touchdown point,
   - Continue a constant approach descent until the landing light reflects on the runway and you can clearly see tire marks.

5. Indications that you might be entering IMC at night include:
   - A disappearance of lights on the ground or stars in the sky.
   - A halo or luminous glow around position lights or a reflection of the landing and anticollision light

6. Calmly, but immediately, reference the flight instruments to initiate a 180°, standard-rate turn to fly out of the weather.